Th

Mickie Mueller is the perfect guide through the looking glass; living the magical life is a reality for her. *The Witch's Mirror* takes one of the most common daily tools and reveals its innate magic. I've been doing spiritual work with mirrors for many years, and this book gave me so many new ways to use them. You'll never look in the mirror the same way again!

> Lunaea Weatherstone, author of *Tending Brigid's Flame* and *Mystical Cats Tarot*

The Witch's Mirror is a lighthearted book that reflects a wide variety of perspectives, techniques, and magickal styles. From faery tales to pop culture and then to modern magickal practice, the mystique of the mirror is revealed.

> Ellen Dugan, author of the Witchery series and *The Natural Psychic*

If you want to know about magic and mirrors, this is the book for you! Mickie Mueller has done an excellent job of researching and bringing together all the many facets of mirror-related beliefs, traditions, and lore.

> Tess Whitehurst, author of *Holistic Energy Magic* and *Magical Housekeeping*

The Witch's Mirror

Mickie Mueller is an award-winning and critically acclaimed artist of fantasy, fairy, and myth. An ordained Pagan minister, Mickie has studied natural magic, fairy magic, and Celtic tradition. She is also a Reiki healing master/teacher in the Usui Shiki Royoho Tradition. Mickie enjoys creating magical art full of fairies, goddesses, and beings of folklore. She works primarily in a mix of colored pencil and watercolor infused with magical herbs corresponding to her subject matter.

Mickie is the illustrator of *The Well Worn Path* and *The Hidden Path* decks, the writer/illustrator of *Voice of the Trees: A Celtic Divination Oracle*, and the illustrator of *The Mystical Cats Tarot*. Since 2007 Mickie has been a regular article and illustration contributor to several of the Llewellyn periodicals. She resides in Missouri.

The Craft, Lore & Magick
of the Looking Glass

The
Witch's
Mirror

Mickie Mueller

Llewellyn Publications
Woodbury, Minnesota

FIRST EDITION
Sixth Printing, 2021
Book design by Rebecca Zins
Cover design by Shira Atakpu
Cover illustration by Mickie Mueller
Interior illustrations by Mickie Mueller
Llewellyn is a registered trademark of Llewellyn Worldwide, Ltd.

Library of Congress Cataloging-in-Publication Data
Names: Mueller, Mickie, 1965– author.
Title: The witch's mirror : the craft, lore, and magic of the looking glass / Mickie Mueller.
Description: FIRST EDITION. | Woodbury : Llewellyn Worldwide Ltd., 2016. | Series: The witch's tools series ; #4 | Includes bibliographical references.
Identifiers: LCCN 2016003001 (print) | LCCN 2016009327 (ebook) | ISBN 9780738747910 | ISBN 9780738748757
Subjects: LCSH: Mirrors—Miscellanea. | Magic. | Witchcraft.
Classification: LCC BF1623.M57 M84 2016 (print) | LCC BF1623.M57 (ebook) |
   DDC 133.4/3—dc23
LC record available at http://lccn.loc.gov/2016003001

Llewellyn Publications
A Division of Llewellyn Worldwide Ltd.
2143 Wooddale Drive
Woodbury, MN 55125-2989
www.llewellyn.com

Printed in the United States of America

THIS BOOK *is dedicated to*
William Vaughan, my grandpa.
He was a scholar, magician,
man of honor, Freemason,
gardener, and crafter of mirrors
for seeing into distant galaxies
and deep into my heart,
always and forever.

contents

Contents

8: Spells for Witch's Mirrors   173

Introduction

The Witch and the Looking Glass

A witch standing before a mirror is a classic icon. Whether it's Snow White's ill-tempered stepmom looking for beauty advice or Harry Potter communing with his long-lost parents, magic mirrors hold a place in our imagination. Of course, these are examples of fictional witches, but real witches have used magical mirrors for ages. The connection with mirrors and witchcraft is very real indeed.

The reflective surfaces of witch's mirrors throughout history have been made from reflecting pools, obsidian, polished copper, brass, and modern glass mirrors both silvered and blackened. One of the most commonly known uses for today's witch's mirror is the art of scrying, or peering into the unknown within a deep reflective surface. In truth, the magic of mirrors doesn't stop there; many witches have various uses for mirrors, including protection, hex breaking, multiplying power, glamour magic, exploring the inner self, meditation, and even improving the energy flow in a home through the art of feng shui.

Some of the most famous mirrors in literature were infused with magical power. Alice stepped through her looking glass into a madcap journey of inner growth. J. R. R. Tolkien wrote of Galadriel and her famous silver basin mirror that shows "many things, and not all have yet come to pass. Some shall never come to be." Perseus used Athena's gift, a magic shield polished to a mirrored finish, to protect himself and safely strike down the gorgon Medusa. We discover through the myths and legends of mirrors that a reflective surface can help us to see deeply within, as well as reach far beyond ourselves.

Today's witch has many mirrors in the home. Most are used to check our reflections—make sure our hair looks perfect, eyebrows plucked, pointy hat on straight—but many witches have magical mirrors tucked away for ritual use as well. The magic mirror can be new or antique, bought or crafted by hand. All are enchanted tools of the trade. You can craft a magic mirror or make any mirror magical by the use of symbols, herbs, oils, condensers, and, of course, your own magical intention.

The art of looking-glass magic is very rewarding, putting you in touch with your own spirit and giving you new ways to manifest abundance, protection, glamour, and divination. Would you like to know how to find, create, and use magical mirrors for scrying, spells, amulets, and more? Well, you now have the secrets of the witch's mirror at your fingertips, so turn the page and gaze into your own magical mirror; what will you discover?

MIRROR LORE
In Chinese tradition,
mirrors frighten away
evil spirits, who are repelled
by their own reflections.

chapter
1

Mirrors in History, Tradition, and Lore

When we think of a mirror, we think of the modern glass mirror with high-definition quality—thin, light, and affordable. Mirrors have been with us in one form or another for ages longer than many people might realize, but they've always been seen as magic. The first mirror was probably a pond or even a puddle that one of our ancient ancestors looked down into and pondered this strange, upside-down world full of trees, clouds, and a curiously familiar human peering back at them. Early village mages also used obsidian mirrors. Obsidian is smooth and reflective volcanic glass, perfect for making a scrying mirror. These mirrors have been around as early as the Neolithic period, and some people still use obsidian scrying mirrors today.

Once people began working with metals, they realized that one of its properties was its ability to reflect; for ages mirrors

Clockwise from top:
Neolithic obsidian,
Roman, and
Egyptian Hathor
mirrors

were actually made out of highly polished copper, brass, and even silver. Versions of metal mirrors were used from the Bronze Age right up through the Middle Ages. There are lots of Greco-Roman vases with paintings of ladies with hand mirrors, including the goddess Venus herself! Fancy metal hand mirrors from ancient Egypt with little figures for the handles have been unearthed over the years. The Romans did a bit of experimenting with glass and lead and made a few glass mirrors, but they were small and not as lovely and clear as what we see today. In Roman times metal mirrors were still much more common.

During the Middle Ages polished metal mirrors were still very popular, but there also were some made of polished rock crystal backed with metal foil, as well as a few very small and highly prized glass mirrors.

Just before the Renaissance, the art of glassmaking was really taking off in Europe. People started making better-quality glass mirrors by using glass-blowing techniques and backing the glass with metals like mercury and silver. These weren't the flat mirrors of today; they were convex mirrors that looked like half of a reflective bubble in a round frame called an *oeil de sorcière*, or sorcerer's eye. These were a popular luxury item; while mostly decorative, they also provided protection from incoming supernatural, menacing forces and bestowed a blessing upon the home. They also earned the name "banker's mirror" due to the wide field of vision they

Mirrors in History, Tradition, and Lore

provided, thus adding extra security both magically and mundanely. The most famous of these is auspiciously placed in the 1434 painting *The Arnolfini Portrait* by Jan van Eyck.

MIRROR LORE
*Many cultures believe that a person's
reflection in a mirror is more than
just a likeness: it reflects their soul.*

By the 1600s craftsmen on the island of Murano in Venice had figured out how to create large, flat glass mirrors with a combination of tin and mercury on the back, and by adding gold and bronze to the mix, the reflection was even more beautiful. These new mirrors were so cool and costly that by the end of the sixteenth century, the who's who of royalty just had to have them—lots of them. They created entire mirrored halls and rooms to impress guests and, I'm sure, also to admire their own awesome reflections. These very extravagant glass mirrors were only affordable to the upper crust.

Just like any new technology, however, if you wait long enough, the price will come down. By the Victorian era most people had glass mirrors in their home, both small hand mirrors and wall mirrors backed with silver, tin, and mercury. In fact, it was during the Victorian era that all sorts of items popped up using mirror-making techniques. Reflective vases, candlesticks, goblets, and more from that era are known as mercury glass.

Most of today's mirrors are backed with aluminum; the process is still called "silvering" even though there's no silver involved. Modern mirrors reflect incoming energies and repel any unwanted vibes as well as their older silver and tin predecessors. Your modern mirror is just the latest in a long line of innovation that is both magical and mundane.

REFLECTIONS OF
REAL WITCHES:
Judika Illes

Death and the Mirror

A widespread funeral tradition demands that mirrors be covered in the room, house, or building where someone has just died. This custom is shared by numerous cultures, religions, and spiritual traditions, so variations exist. Some find it appropriate to use the first thing at hand: towels, sheets, tablecloths, or clothing. Formal Victorian mourning etiquette, on the other hand, recommended draping black velvet over mirrors. Meanwhile, others prevent mirrors from reflecting by turning them to face a wall.

All sorts of modern rationales explain this practice, but the tradition of covering mirrors in the presence of death is ancient and deeply rooted in magic and mysticism. It is a response to the mirror's traditional roles as a soul catcher and as a portal to other realms. Covering a mirror serves two essential goals: to protect the living and to protect the dead.

When a crystal ball is not in active use, it's customary to cover it, typically with velvet, silk, or other fine fabric. Covering a crystal ball allows it to rest, but it also temporarily closes the portal it provides. Veiling a mirror is akin to covering a crystal ball. When Death is in the house, it's considered unwise to leave those portals open.

The threshold that exists from the moment of death until the soul's arrival at its next destination (Summerlands, Avalon, Heaven, Valhalla, and so forth) is considered especially treacherous. Vigilant rituals, such as covering mirrors, attempt to ensure that the dead rest in peace. It is feared that a soul, potentially disoriented immediately after dying, might somehow become trapped within a mirror. Alternatively, some fear that the spirits who dwell within mirrors may use these portals to lure newly dead souls into their realm. Either way, the uncovered mirror potentially disrupts the desired journey to the next realm. Once trapped in the mirror, the frustrated soul may wreak havoc upon the living. Extraction may be challenging and dangerous. Covering the mirror protects the newly dead as well as prevents residual hauntings.

Judika Illes
**author of *The Encyclopedia of 5000 Spells*,
Encyclopedia of Witchcraft, and other books
of magic • judikailles.com**

Mirror Lore and Superstitions

From the first time Greek hottie Narcissus fell in love with his reflection in a pool, mirrors have been equally treasured and feared for their strange reflective properties. Many superstitions seem to stem from the perception of a mirror as a passageway between worlds.

Let's look at some of the classic and sometimes contradictory superstitions regarding mirrors. Watch for more throughout this book.

- If you break a mirror, you will have seven years of bad luck. One cure for this is to bury the pieces of the mirror.

- Many cultures believe that covering mirrors in the house where someone has died prevented the capture of the soul of the departed within the mirror or preventing the dead from returning through the mirror, depending on the culture.

- It's bad luck to receive a mirror as a gift from the home of someone who is deceased.

- A mirror falling from a wall is said to predict an impending death in the family.

- If a couple looks at their reflections together in a mirror on their wedding day, they will have a happy marriage.

- Some cultures believed that allowing a baby to see their own reflection before their first birthday would cause death.

- Eating an apple while brushing your hair at midnight and looking into a mirror, you will see either your future spouse or the Grim Reaper.

- It's bad luck to see your reflection in a mirror by candlelight. (It does make you look kind of creepy, so maybe that's why.)

- A vampire will have no reflection in a mirror.

- In the Middle Ages women were warned that primping too long before a mirror would cause them to see the devil himself there and go mad.

Yes, the mirror does hold its mysteries and has kept people on their toes for centuries. I'm sure the adolescent daughters of medieval lords responded with huge eye rolls when warned of the evils of mirrors.

Legends and Lore of the Witch's Magical Mirror

Witches' association with mirrors makes sense: witches walk between the worlds, and the mirror has long been regarded as a passageway to other worlds. Gazing into a mirror in order to see secrets of the past, present, or future is known as the art of catoptromancy, one of the first uses of the magic mirror. There were priests in ancient Rome, Greece, and Egypt who included the art of gazing into mirrors of obsidian or polished metal among the magical arsenal they used to learn secrets beyond normal perception. Modern witches call this form of divination *seeing* or *scrying*. The term *scrying* comes from the Middle English word *descry*, meaning "to catch sight of something difficult to see." Both scrying mirrors and other forms of magic mirrors permeate history.

The Chinese developed a special kind of armor known as mirror armor, which is made of large convex metal mirrors that would fit over a soldier's regular armor. The metal disks not only deflected the physical threat of sword blades and arrows, but they also repelled psychic attack and demons. These mirrors were usually worn over the chest, back, and upper arms. Another Eastern magic mirror is the *melong*, a large metal convex mirror that is worn over the chest by the Tibetan Nechung oracle as part of his regalia. The Nechung that wears it is a simple Tibetan monk who specializes in channeling visions for the Dalai Lama. (Yep, even the Dalai Lama uses a magic mirror!)

In India and Pakistan mirrors have been used as magical embellishments for ages. Shisha embroidery is the art of attaching tiny mirrors to clothing and dowry textiles, decorative objects, and walls to bring blessings of good fortune. The fancy Indian decorative door hanging known as the toran is covered with tiny mirrors. Torans have a glittering row of embroidered and mirror-decorated pointed leaflike shapes that hang down. These hangings are meant to fill the home with blessings of protection and fertility; additionally, they reflect sunlight, which repels the evil eye. These mirrored toran decorations were used as magical protection for a married couple and were a valued part of a bride's dowry.

How about a "death ray" using mirrors? Ancient Greek mathematician and technologist Archimedes thought it would be a great idea. Although the accounts vary on exactly how he did it, legend says the Roman fleet that was sailing in to conquer Syracuse was foiled by the seventy-year-old Archimedes, who would protect his hometown with his greatest resource: his mighty brain. His plan involved giant mirrors that were set up along the shore. He reportedly reflected the sun's rays at the Roman galleys, setting them ablaze. Many since have tested this legend and failed, including the Discovery Channel's *Mythbusters,* who tried it in both seasons one and three but never managed to confirm the myth. Apparently a team of researchers at MIT worked on the problem and did manage to burst a ship into flames; however, it was a completely motionless ship, not one rocking in the ocean. The legend of Archimedes' burning mirrors still captures the imagination. Did he manage to do it or did he simply blind them with science?

Italian-born queen and regent of France Catherine de' Medici was said to own more than one magic mirror, and it's speculated that she used mirrors for both scrying and magic spells. Famous contemporary (and sometimes cohort of de' Medici) was the seer Nostradamus. He used a bowl of water or dark ink as a scrying mirror to reveal his insights into future events, which he wrote down as poetic prose. Nostradamus's predictions still shake people up from time to time. When

Mirrors in History, Tradition, and Lore

Nostradamus died, Catherine de' Medici reportedly continued working with magic mirrors on her own, thus earning her the unofficial title of "queen witch."

De' Medici was not the only queen of the time to consult a magic mirror. Queen Elizabeth I consulted with Dr. John Dee, her own court magician and astrologer. Dee and his colleague Edward Kelley utilized a concave onyx mirror described in a satirical poem by Samuel Butler as "the devil's looking-glass." It's said that the mirror was used both for scrying and to summon spirits. Queen Elizabeth consulted Dee in many matters of state and considered him a trusted and respected servant of the throne. The onyx mirror Dee used to serve queen and country can be seen today in the British Museum.

John Dee's work with his onyx speculum is his most famous association with mirror magic, but, in fact, Dee also studied the reflections within silvered mirrors of his time as part of his metaphysical study of optics (or, as he referred to it, "perspective"). Dee believed that mirrors were the perfect way to contemplate spiritual reality. He asserted that by learning how mirrors worked, we could learn to see through deceptions that are placed before our eyes. Upon receiving a mirror as a gift from Sir William Pickering, Dee marveled at how his reflection appeared as he lunged at himself, dagger in hand, as the mirror battle appeared real to his view. Dee's exploration into the magic mirror sent up a buzz of constant rumors about him partnering with the devil, and it's rumored that Dee was at least partial inspiration for such literary characters of the time as Doctor Faustus (as imagined by Marlowe) and Prospero (from Shakespeare's *The Tempest*).

Paschal Beverly Randolph was a spiritualist during the 1800s who published many books, several regarding the use of magic mirrors. He studied many forms of magic and divination under several esoteric orders. Mirror work was included in his studies, and he expanded upon that work by making mirrors of his own and importing magic mirrors from India. Some of his published works explain use of fluid condensers for scrying mirrors. Randolph's practice was guided by his perception of a connection between science and the occult. His books on magic mirrors are still highly regarded by modern witches.

Victorian Spiritualists in England had a technique using a large magic mirror in the confines of a very small darkened room or booth draped in black fabric and very low light for contacting spirits of the deceased through a séance of sorts. This small room with a mirror in it was known as a psychomanteum. It's believed that the Victorians were reviving the technique based on an old Greek method in which oracles would stare into a pool of water in a dark room. The psychomanteum method has been carried over into recent times by the works of Dr. Raymond Moody.

Franz Bardon was a Czechoslovakian Spiritualist who worked extensively with magic mirrors and other esoteric studies. Bardon wrote several books in the 1950s about mysticism and Hermetics, and included were his formulas for creating fluid condensers and working with scrying mirrors, which I'll explain later on. Bardon held his spirituality sacred and survived being imprisoned in a Nazi concentration camp for refusing to use his knowledge of mysticism to help the Nazi cause. His knowledge of fluid condensers used for mirrors and other magical purposes is highly regarded by practitioners to this day.

There are a few sought-after wooden-framed witch mirrors floating around out there from the mid-nineteenth century that were made in Belfast. Famous witch Doreen Valiente herself owned one of these charming mirrors. There's also one in the Museum of Witchcraft in Boscastle, Cornwall. The frame is a woodcarving of an impish-looking witch, legs crossed at her ankles, elbows on her knees, and a curvy hat above her mischievous face. The silvered mirror looks as though the witch has wrapped her body around the mirror itself. It is said that a familiar spirit has made its home within the mirror and may be seen standing behind you and communicating with you if you gaze into the mirror. There is a warning that if it creeps you out too much, just close your eyes, but do not turn around! Why not? I'm not sure I want to know. That being said, I would try it if I ever had the opportunity.

Occasionally you'll find magic workers even today who harbor suspicions of mirror magic for various reasons, probably stemming from a belief that mirror magic is only good for negative magic, but as we will explore in this book, nothing could be further from the truth. Taboos and superstitions against mirrors go back as far as the mirror itself, but at the end of the day, as far as mirror magic goes, it's just a tool like any other tool. If a clever witch uses mirrors with respect, understanding, and care, the magic mirror can become a valued part of any magical tool bag.

MIRROR LORE
*In Persian lore, sitting very still
and combing your hair in front of a
mirror without speaking will allow
you to see ghosts in the reflection.*

Mirror Deities

Did you know there are lots of deities associated with mirrors? Here are just a few selected mirror deities and their fascinating stories.

Venus and Aphrodite

The beautiful goddess of love, beauty, and sexuality is known as Venus by the Romans and associated with the Greek goddess Aphrodite. And yes, she's the only goddess to have a planet named after her. The same symbol representing the goddess Venus, her planet, and the feminine gender is a representation of an old Roman bronze hand mirror: ♀.

There are many ancient Greek depictions on pottery of Aphrodite holding a hand mirror. Myriad classical paintings of her during the Renaissance period portray Venus gazing into a mirror. In many of these pieces, upon first inspection it may seem that she is admiring her own beauty, but where are her eyes actually looking? You realize that the mirror is, in fact, angled so the goddess is looking at you, the viewer. This is known as the "Venus effect."

Paulo Coelho reminds us of this: "The eyes are the mirror of the soul and reflect everything that seems to be hidden; and like a mirror, they also reflect the person looking into them."

Hathor

Another goddess of beauty, Hathor is a pre-dynastic Egyptian goddess with mirror associations. Granted, Hathor is a complex goddess—she has been associated with dancing, drinking, music, and even providing hospitality for the dead—but before such activities, you've got to get ready. Hathor's association with mirrors includes her role as a patroness of cosmetics and perfume. The Egyptians were known for being well appointed, and their use of cosmetics was renowned in the ancient world. You can't apply cosmetics without a mirror (well, you can, but it's ill advised).

The hand mirrors and makeup palettes used by the Egyptians often depicted the lovely cow-eared face of this goddess. Her sacred stones, malachite and turquoise, were favorites used in Egypt to make cosmetics. Hathor was not a shallow goddess, though; she also saw the beauty inside. According to Judika Illes, Hathor's "traditional votive offering was two mirrors, the better with which to see both her beauty and your own."

Ishikore-dome

In the Shinto religion of Japan, Ishikore-dome is an androgynous or transgender deity of the arts and quality craftsmanship who is credited with the invention of the mirror. This

Mirrors in History, Tradition, and Lore

fabulous deity had the creative skills to cheer up the sun goddess Amaterasu herself.

According to legend, Amaterasu had become sullen after a horrible battle with her brother, the storm god, and retreated to a cave, keeping her light from the world. Ishikore-dome found a solution by crafting a beautiful mirror made of stone and copper. The goddess of dance came out to the cave entrance and put on a bawdy show that was so entertaining that the cheering and laughter of the other gods and goddesses lured the sun goddess Amaterasu out of her cave to see what all the fuss was about. The sun then became captivated by her shining reflection in Ishikore-dome's magical mirror, and the other deities were able to seal the cave. The sun returned to the world and cast her warming light upon the land, bringing joy and spring.

Tezcatlipoca

The Aztecs who made gleaming obsidian mirrors had Tezcatlipoca, also known as the Lord of the Smoking Mirror, to guide them in their gazing. He might have a dark-sounding name, and for good reason: he ruled over the first four worlds that came before this one (this guy's seen a lot of destruction). Tezcatlipoca is one of about 130 different aspects of this complex deity. In his "smoking mirror" form, he's often represented with a black stripe across his face, as seen on the famous mask that had been worn by his priests, now housed in the British Museum along with an Aztec obsidian mirror.

A black mirror or "smoking mirror" is usually part of his likenesses, either as part of his headdress, worn on his chest, or in place of a torn-off foot. The word for mirror was the same as the word for ruler, which is telling in the relationship the people had with these obsidian mirrors. The smoking mirror had a dualistic nature, both a receiver of divine communication and a transmitter, much the way that the human eye sees and judges its surroundings but is also considered a window to the soul. To gaze within the all-seeing eye of Tezcatlipoca's smoking mirror was to communicate back and forth with the deity himself. He saw everything in that smoking mirror and knew everything that was done or thought by his people—everything seen and unseen. He was a protector of slaves and punished wrongdoers. (While that may sound nice, he also enjoyed a yearly human sacrifice.)

MIRROR LORE

According to an old wives' tale,
mirrors should be covered during
a thunderstorm to keep them
from attracting lightning.

Blake Octavian Blair

Shamanic Magic Mirrors

Shamanism holds some lore of its own to add to the milieu of the magic mirror. Shamanic traditions from Mongolia and the Buryat region use a highly polished metal disc called a *toli* as a mirror. Tolis serve many functions, including warding off malevolent entities, scrying and divination, and healing through various ceremonial procedures. The toli is occasionally used by some practitioners as a portal for the shaman's compassionate helping spirits to enter and exit a ceremonial space. The empowered toli is placed upon the shaman's altar, and as they are called or needed, the spirits enter and exit the ceremony and healing session through the toli, which serves as focal point of power. As is common with tools in many branches of mystical spirituality, not only will different shamanic cultures use the mirror in different ways, but even within a culture the way a toli is used may vary from practitioner to practitioner.

Another form of magic mirror almost all of us have readily available access to is water. An old standby form of magic mirror is simply a large bowl of clear water. Create a dimly lit sacred space, fill a large basin with water, focus on your question at hand, and note the images that appear to you in the water's silvery surface. It's trusted, tried, true, and at your fingertips.

Blessed be!

Blake Octavian Blair
**Pagan, author, ordained minister, shamanic practitioner, Usui Reiki Master-Teacher, tarot reader, and musician •
www.blakeoctavianblair.com**

Mirrors in History, Tradition, and Lore

chapter
2

Magical Mirrors
in Popular Culture

The witch's mirror has captured our imagination and earned its place in popular culture, especially in books, film, and television.

Probably the magic mirror that most often pops to mind is the mirror of the Wicked Queen from Disney's animated classic *Snow White and the Seven Dwarfs,* based on the classic Grimm's fairy tale. We immediately envision her, with black and purple swirling around her, vainly demanding her question: "Magic mirror on the wall, who is the fairest one of all?" Obsessed with her own reflection, she questioned the familiar spirit housed in her magic mirror to constantly compare her own appearance with all other women in the land. If she would have done some mirror work to look within herself instead of focusing just on her looks, she might have been a happier person and not come to such a sticky end.

Another well-known story is the charming sequel to *Alice's Adventures in Wonderland*, *Alice Through the Looking Glass*. Here we find Alice on her second adventure to a mystical realm as she climbs through a magical looking glass into a magical land of self-discovery. Alice's adventure into a backwards land can be seen as a metaphor for a shamanic journey to discover her own identity and her place in the world. She discovers backwards poetry that only can be read in a mirror. Other things are done backwards in this land, like passing out a cake and then cutting it, characters remembering the future, and Alice having to travel in the opposite direction of where she wants to go. She meets many interesting characters as she traverses the inversed logic and physics of this strange mirror world and learns about herself and her place in life along the way. She also learns that she has to follow certain rules through chess imagery. Upon returning to the mundane world, she brings with her much more personal power than she had at the beginning of her magical experience.

A modern coming-of-age story using a mystical mirror is the 2005 film *MirrorMask*. Written by Neil Gaiman and Dave McKean, this fantasy film involves a mysterious world, double identities, and an elusive reflective mask that is the key to everything. When fifteen-year-old Helena's mother ends up being hospitalized for an unexplained illness, Helena finds herself magically transported into the fantastic city she's created from her emotionally charged art. Fish fly through the air, books are alive, and—well, it's Dave McKean. If you've ever seen the Sandman comic books, it's his imagination but in film. The MirrorMask is a charm symbolic of Helena's inspiration to create the city on both sides of the sheets of paper, a city of both light and shadow. The MirrorMask has other mysterious powers that are revealed as the story unfolds… no spoilers!

MIRROR LORE
Some people say if you fall asleep
in front of a mirror, your soul
might get confused by the reflection
and enter the mirror rather than
your body before you awake.

Another famous mirror was probably in your own bathroom, as it was in mine in my preadolescent years: the mirror of Bloody Mary! Yes, any mirror lit only by candlelight becomes a portal to terror when awakened with that well-known charm from urban legend. With the repeated chant of "Bloody Mary, Bloody Mary, Bloody Mary," she appears and scares the bejeezus out of tweens everywhere! I spent many sleepover parties with all the guests, packed tightly into the darkened bathroom, chanting "Bloody Mary" by candlelight. The ritual always ended the same way: piercing screams and pajama-clad preteens bursting through the bathroom door like bullets from a gun. We knew we all had seen her and had barely survived being murdered or disfigured, as the legend implied!

Who was Bloody Mary? Queen Mary I, who had burned Protestants at the stake, was dubbed Bloody Mary for her cruel executions. Many people believe the childhood game evolved from her cruel history.

A variation on the Bloody Mary urban legend is Mary Worth. Much like Bloody Mary, you stand in front of a mirror in the dark, lit only by a candle. The repeating charm for summoning Mary Worth is: "Mary Worth, I took your baby!" I don't know about you, but I don't plan on taunting a dark spirit on the other side of a candlelit mirror in such a way, urban legend or not! There are many versions of this legend; some say the woman appearing in the mirror is a woman who killed her children or other people's children or even that she's a witch (ahem)!

How do these childhood tests of bravery work? Often the chanting includes spinning as well; then, when the person looks in the mirror with their face lit only by candlelight, their own face—already screwed into a fearful expression—appears to be unrecognizable. Cue scared kids screaming and running from the bathroom. Oh, good times!

These terrifying mirror rituals have become so pervasive that many savvy film and TV writers have used the element to haunt our adulthood too. In the 1992 film *Candyman* the mirror chant would summon forth an African American portrait artist seeking revenge for his tortured death by a mob. Man, never get on an artist's bad side.

American Horror Story got on the bathroom mirror bandwagon in season 1, episode 6, "Piggy Piggy." This episode offered several "jump scares" in their version of the monster in the mirror theme. The misguided therapist Ben convinces his patient to face his fears of a Bloody Mary–inspired urban legend. This dark being beyond the mirror was Piggy Man, a Chicago hog butcher wearing a grisly mask made from one of his hogs.

Supernatural is another TV series to explore Bloody Mary. In this version it's discovered that Bloody Mary is actually traveling through mirrors and exacting revenge on people close to the summoner who've victimized people in their lives. Seeing it took me right back to those thrilling sleepovers scaring each other with the bathroom mirror.

These stories and films really do haunt many people in a serious way. When I began researching this book, I was surprised to discover how deep people's superstitions about monsters in mirrors really run. There are a lot more people who are afraid of mirrors than I ever realized. I discovered chat boards where people talked about their fears. A fellow office worker had a mirror on their desk, so of course they must be doing black magic, right? Someone else said they have to cover all their mirrors at night. Many people just said something like "mirrors are just creepy." Do you think people are afraid of black cats? Well, mirrors really freak some people out too.

There are fears and then there are phobias. The phobia associated most commonly with mirrors is known as catoptrophobia, also known as eisotrophobia, which is more specifically the fear seeing of one's own reflection. Sometimes spectrophobia is associated with a fear of mirrors, but it's really not the mirror causing the fear, it's the fear of what supernatural being may be lurking within its reflective surface, bringing us back to the idea of a mirror as a portal. In the instance of a phobia, seeing mirrors can be quite crippling, causing full-blown anxiety attacks and other serious symptoms.

MIRROR LORE
Actors believe that seeing their
reflection while looking over someone
else's shoulder is bad luck.

Mirrors in film and literature aren't all scary. One of my all-time favorite magic mirrors comes from the brilliant mind of J. R. R. Tolkien. Tolkien surely used his knowledge and understanding of myths and legends when he wrote about Galadriel, the Elven Lady of Lórien, and her mirror of water and silver. The Mirror of Galadriel was used as an oracle in his book *The Fellowship of the Ring*, from the Lord of the Rings trilogy. The Elven Lady pours the water into the silver basin, creating a magical surface for viewing "many things, and not all have yet come to pass. Some never come to be, unless those that behold the visions turn aside from their path to prevent them."

I remember being enchanted by Galadriel's mirror in the Ralph Bakshi animated film version *Lord of the Rings* in the '70s, and I fell in love all over again when I saw it in the Peter Jackson version of *The Fellowship of the Ring*. Many notable visionary artists have portrayed this most elegant magical water mirror, including the Bros. Hildebrandt, Raoul Vitale, and Alan Lee. Did you ever pretend that your bird bath was Galadriel's mirror? (You know you did; I did too.)

The realms of fantasy are filled with magic mirrors, and J. K. Rowling's world of witches and wizards is no exception. There are several magic mirrors in the world of the Harry Potter books and films, the most memorable being the Mirror of Erised, an addictive mirror that reflects your heart's desire. Hidden away in a dark, unused hall at Hogwarts, Harry finds

Magical Mirrors in Popular Culture

it and uses it to spend time with his parents, who were killed when he was just a baby, as their reflections are manifested within the giant framed mirror. In the Harry Potter world there are also pairs of two-way mirrors, each connected to the other. They're used for communication, sort of like Skype, using magic.

Another portal type of magical mirror comes from the 1756 fairy tale *Beauty and the Beast* by Jeanne-Marie Leprince de Beaumont. The heroine of the story, Belle (the French word for "beauty"), is forced to live in the castle of a strange beast as restitution for her father's thievery of a rose. The two develop a friendship (whether through the beast's kindness or Stockholm syndrome), and when the beast eventually releases her, he gives her a magic hand mirror that she can use as a portal to see what is going on at the beast's castle and a ring that can magically return her there. Many of us are most familiar with the Disney version of this story, which has always been among my favorites, and that magic mirror has been a key element to the story going all the way back to its original version.

The film *The Skeleton Key* is a supernatural thriller that utilizes hoodoo as a main element of the story, and superstitions regarding mirrors are introduced throughout. When live-in caregiver Caroline first comes to stay at a former plantation home in the Louisiana bayou, she thinks the fact that elderly Violet's aversion to mirrors in the house is just an eccentricity. She later learns that it holds much deeper implications. She discovers too late that mirrors have a powerful connection to the soul, especially when a hoodoo ritual using a large mirror is performed. Dear witches, keep in mind that while the film is full of actual hoodoo elements because the filmmakers were very well-advised by Catherine Yronwode (as an uncredited consultant), this is not a hoodoo training film and much of the magic in it is not real—it's not meant to be, but it's a fun and scary movie all the same.

Pretty much every vampire in popular culture, whether in books, film, comics, even cartoons, has a thing with mirrors. Bram Stoker's knowledge and research into the Eastern European folklore before writing his novel *Dracula* brought the fictional bloodsuckers' catoptrophobia (the fear of mirrors) into popular culture. In the novel, Jonathan Harker uses his own shaving mirror, since there are none in Dracula's home, and discovers by accident that the strange Count does not, in fact, have a reflection. Dracula then calls the mirror a "bauble of vanity" and smashes it. Dracula helped forge the legends of horror-genre vampires for generations to come; from Anne Rice's *Interview with a Vampire* to BBC's *Being Human,* most (but not all) literary and film vampires have no reflection.

The first season of the series *Heroes,* inspired by comic book–style storytelling, introduced a story arc involving a character who discovered her superpower through her own reflection in mirrors and other reflective surfaces. Niki

Sanders, like most of the other main characters in this sci-fi/ fantasy drama, has unusual abilities, but her power is only active when her alter ego Jessica takes over. When the going gets tough, Niki sees her dark side, known as Jessica, through her own reflection. When Niki and Jessica switch places, Niki becomes trapped within the reflective world while she watches Jessica, who has the power of super strength, take over. In most situations Jessica generally wreaks havoc and then leaves Niki to clean up the proverbial and/or literal mess afterwards. Perhaps this storyline points to our feelings about our own dark sides lurking on the other side of the looking glass.

Clearly, the mainstream has been inspired by the old legends, superstitions, and curiosity surrounding the magical mirror, which allows the mystery of mirrors to permeate our culture.

MIRROR LORE
A cure for the seven years of bad
luck a broken mirror brings is to
take one of the shards to a cemetery
and touch it to a headstone.

Chapter 2

Natalie Zaman

Shattering Superstition:
The Magic of Broken Mirrors

Look into a broken mirror and you will see yourself and the world around you from different perspectives and in bits and pieces—the parts rather than the sum of the whole that you would find reflected in intact glass. The minute is brought into focus, and then, depending on the angle of your gaze, doubled or multiplied a thousand times—which makes for some seriously potent magic. One of my favorite ways to work with mirror fragments is to use them to multiply and intensify the energy of a crystal grid.

Even without scent, the shapes and colors of certain flowers evoke powerful emotions and energies for me. They have inspired many of my crystal layouts, and incorporating mirror shards into my grids has enhanced the magic I've manifested with them. As an example, picturing a sunflower as a project for which I wanted to cultivate brilliant success, I used protective black tourmaline nuggets to form the flower's center (the sunflower's head is where its seeds, or future growth, are created). Alternating clear quartz and citrine points brought creativity, optimism, abundance, and clarity to the grid and represented the flower's petals. Tumbled pieces of malachite (for banishing negative thoughts and removing stumbling blocks) and turquoise (for growth and healing) formed the stem and leaves. Reflected by the glass underneath, the working was present in this world and in those existing in each mirror, magnifying it and multiplying its energy and intention into infinity. I found myself getting help for my work from all quarters.

The next time you encounter a broken mirror—by chance or by your own hand—save the pieces! (Remember that the edges of the glass may be jagged and very sharp. Work slowly and carefully whenever you handle them to avoid injury.) Mirrors, even broken ones, are potential portals to other worlds, so it's important to cleanse every shard that will be used for magical work.

To cleanse them, lay out all of the pieces on a black cloth, then sprinkle them with water to which three measures of salt have been added. As you work, state your intention: *I clear these portals with water and earth.* Next, light a stick of your favorite incense and smudge the pieces, again with an intention: *I clear these portals with fire and air.* Finally, charge the fragments with your Spirit. Breathe on each one, thinking or speaking aloud: *May the magic worked through this glass be for my highest and greatest good*. Flip the pieces over and do the same on the reverse side.

When you have cleansed and charged your mirror pieces, arrange them into the shape of your choice: intersecting lines for working with crossroads, directional or elemental energies, labyrinths and spirals for pathworking, or any symbol that holds meaning for you or as your crystals direct when you handle them. As you work with stones and mirror fragments in tandem, you'll find the method and rhythm for placement that is right for you. Once your pattern is complete, simply place your stones on top of the glass fragments. You can set the shards permanently into a base or tabletop, but I prefer to keep them loose for the flexibility to create new and ever-evolving grids.

What shape will your shards take?

Natalie Zaman
**Co-author of Graven Images Oracle deck,
writer for *FATE*, *SageWoman*, and *newWitch*,
and writes the feature "Wandering Witch"
for *Witches and Pagans* • http://nataliezaman.com,
http://broomstix.blogspot.com**

Magical Mirrors in Popular Culture

chapter
3

Which Mirrors
for Witch's Mirrors?

There are many kinds of mirrors, so how will you possibly know where to begin looking for your own witch's mirror? What attributes does each kind of mirror have? Which mirror works best for the kind of magic you will be doing? Never fear: this chapter is your jumping-off point! Let's take a look at the different kinds of witch's mirrors and enchanted looking glasses and learn the reasons for different kinds of mirrors and how the size, shape, and even the curve of the mirror's surface indicates the best magical use for each.

You can buy mirrors and enchant them for your magical purpose, you can make your own, or you can add your own crafty and artistically witchy elements to a storebought mirror, making it unique. Whether you want your mirror to be a hands-on project from start to finish or you prefer to purchase a gorgeous mirror and enchant it for your purpose, you need to know about the different kinds of mirrors and what magical powers they possess.

Silver Mirror, Black Mirror

The two most common colors you'll see of glass witch's mirrors are black and silver. Both types of mirror are made out of glass, with the difference being the kind of coating on the back of the mirror.

Silver Mirrors

While modern silver mirrors don't have actual silver in the reflective coating like some antique ones do, the modern counterparts are still referred to as silver, and the coating on the back of the glass is called "silvering" as a reference to the original method of making glass mirrors with shiny, reflective silver or mercury backs.

Silver mirrors, whether antique or modern, are associated with the full moon, the Mother Goddess, sunlit water, beauty, and self-esteem. A silver mirror is typically used for magic to multiply, reflect, send energy, protect, beautify, and more. Silver mirrors can reflect or draw in positive or negative energy, depending on how you choose to enchant it with your own magical intention.

Black Mirrors

Black mirrors are exactly what they sound like: a clear glass surface with the back coated in black instead of silver. A black mirror offers an entirely different kind of reflective surface than a silver mirror does. You wouldn't want to try to fix your eyeliner in the reflection of a black mirror—you'd likely poke yourself right in the eye! Nope, it's not *that* kind of mirror.

What kind of mirror is it, you ask? A black mirror is a primal thing harkening back to the ancient obsidian mirrors, full of deep mystery, and the darkened pools where the Greeks talked to spirits. Black mirrors are designed to mimic those reflecting pools of old, which were the first mirrors. When modern landscapers set up artificial reflecting pools, the inside is usually black, as this creates a more natural-looking pool with lovely, deep reflections.

The most common use for a black mirror is scrying, but it can also be used for viewing past lives, astral travel, contacting spirits, or remote viewing. The mirror can be set up on a stand or easel facing the viewer, or it can be laid flat on the workspace as a reminder of its watery counterpart. Fancy black mirrors are available in most metaphysical shops and online. A black mirror is also pretty simple to create yourself, as I'll discuss in chapter 6.

Using the psychomanteum technique, both black scrying mirrors and silver mirrors can be used to communicate with those who have passed on to the next world.

REFLECTIONS OF
REAL WITCHES:
Charlynn Walls

Using a Witch's Scrying Mirror

The witch's mirror is an invaluable tool that is versatile in how a person can adapt it to their own personal use. My personal preference is to utilize my own for scrying or for meditative work during the dark of the moon, which is a good time to reveal what is hidden from view or explore what is just below the surface of our conscious self.

In order to see what is obscured from my sight, I set up my altar in a way that is conducive to a meditative state of mind. I want to be as comfortable as possible in order to easily slip into the proper frame of mind. I set up the mirror so that it is comfortably at eye level. I also set out a journal and pen so I can record anything that I glimpse in the reflection of my mirror.

Burning a bit of sandalwood is beneficial to help me focus and create the magickal mindset. I also get a black candle to set off to the side, where I can just catch a glimpse of it. I then try to look past that point into the center of the mirror. The slight flicker of the candlelight and wisps of smoke reflected in the surface of the mirror often help produce some of the more recognizable images that I can then begin to decipher and record for future interpretation.

The mirror is an instrument that is often underutilized, but it is one that can be very powerful when used correctly. In it we access our higher self to divine what is to come or to contemplate situations that need more consideration. Its use allows us to see beyond what is available to our ordinary senses.

Charlynn Walls
**Writes for Llewellyn annuals
and teaches workshops
on a variety of topics •
www.sageofferings.net**

Images in the Mirror May Be Closer Than They Appear

A mirror's shape can have quite a bit of bearing on its best purpose for magical use. While there is some leeway for personal taste and availability, it's important to know the basics. Each shape has a magical correspondence, so if you know that before you choose a mirror, you can take advantage of the shape of the mirror you already own or choose the best mirror for the witchy job.

Round and Oval

Oneness is the key word to remember when using a mirror that is round or oval, the shapes some of the oldest mirrors took. A round- or oval-shaped mirror is generally associated with the eye, even if the oval is up and down. This shape can also be associated with the circle of life, cycles, and unity. A round mirror can represent love. The shape of the mirror represented in the Venus symbol is round, and a round mirror can also remind us of the sun, the moon, or a watchful eye looking out for us. It can also be symbolic of a never-ending ring, representing commitment. A round mirror is an expression of the magic circle.

It's been suggested that the ankh, the Egyptian symbol for life, looks very much like a round- or oval-shaped hand mirror. The long name for mirror in the ancient Egyptian language is *ankh-en-maa-her*, which, according to mirror historian

Mark Pendergrast, may be roughly translated as "life force for seeing the face." That doesn't seem like a coincidence.

A round or oval mirror is great for scrying and meditation; as a magical protection amulet to deflect the evil eye, watch for threats, and bestow blessings; for communication with a lover; for creating harmony in the home; for beauty magic; for spirit communication; and for self-improvement magic.

MIRROR LORE
The Chinese longevity symbol on
a mirror in a gold frame serves
as protection from accidents
and promotes a long life.

Square and Rectangle

Balance is the strength of a square- or rectangular-shaped mirror. A mirror with right angles, such as a square- or rectangle-shaped mirror, is a mirror that puts you in a position of control over situations. Squares and rectangles are a shape of authority, representing the human ability to build and forge society through architecture. Working with a mirror made of right angles can allow you to remain grounded and solid, keeping your magical workings firmly in check. It's a reliable, strong earthy shape for control over any situation. A square mirror can be easily aligned with the four elements and cardinal directions in the traditions of modern witchcraft.

Place a square- or rectangle-shaped mirror in the house to firmly expel any energies not in accord with your greater good; to raise your self esteem; for manifesting; for stability; for legal matters; to communicate with a friend; or for magic to help strengthen communities such as families or covens.

Octagon

Extra power is the benefit that an octagon-shaped mirror offers. Commonly seen in the art of feng shui, the octogon's eight sides represent the four cardinal directions plus the four secondary directions, much like a compass rosette star. An octagonal mirror can attract and expand energy and power. Beyond the feng shui applications, an octagon-shaped mirror can represent the Wheel of the Year, as the eight sides are equal to the eight witch's sabbats. Another symbolic use would be stopping energies you don't want—after all, an octagonal mirror is the same shape as a stop sign.

Magic uses for an octagon-shaped mirror include stopping negative energy, bringing harmony, and boosting power. The octagon shape offers strength, balances karma, creates stability, and boosts health, prosperity, and goodwill.

Concave vs. Convex

The shape a mirror is cut in is one thing, but there are also some mirrors that have a curve to their surfaces; we call that curve either convex or concave. Think of a round bowl. If you set it on the table and look inside the bowl, you're looking at a concave surface. (I use the word "cave" to help me remember the difference. It goes inward, like a cave.) Now, if you turn the bowl over on the table so that the rim is flat on the table and you're looking at the bottom of the bowl, you're looking at a convex surface. (Just remember, if your cereal gets spilled upside down, you'll be vexed.)

That's how I remember the difference between concave and convex. Read on for the magical uses of these specific types of curved mirrors.

Concave Mirrors

A concave mirror draws light, images, and energy inward. Its reflective surface is bent to pull in light, reflections, and therefore energy. A concave mirror is the kind of mirror that we see used for telescopes, as they bend the light inward. Makeup and shaving mirrors are sometimes concave; objects in these mirrors are actually farther away than they appear to be but everything seems closer in the reflection, which makes the work of putting on your makeup or shaving more precise. But these are practical implications of concave mirrors—what about the metaphysical properties?

• • •
Which Mirrors for Witch's Mirrors?

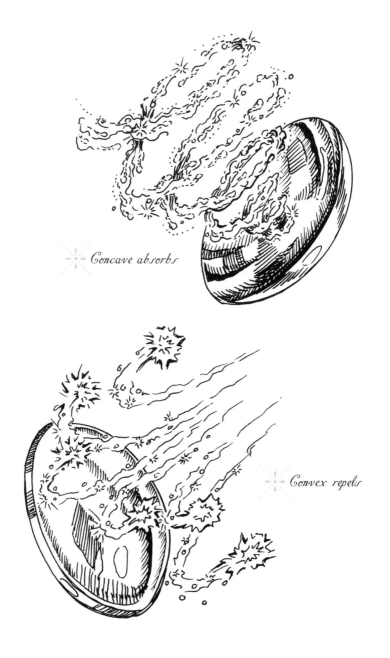

Concave absorbs

Convex repels

A silver concave mirror is great for drawing in any kind of energy. You can enchant a special kind of concave magical mirror that you can use for absorbing and trapping negative energies or entities. You can use this kind of mirror to absorb and neutralize harmful energies sent your way. You can also use a silver concave mirror to draw in and magnify positive energy. For instance, if you own one of those round two-way lighted makeup mirrors, when you're not using it, flip the concave side toward the wall, where you've placed a picture of something you want to draw into your life. That's quick and easy mirror magic—powerfully simple.

Some black mirrors used for scrying are concave. Because of the curved shape, the black of the mirror reflects more of itself in the surface, creating a very deep black mirror for concentrating on while scrying, astral traveling, or communicating with spirits. As you gaze into a concave black mirror, it pulls your gaze further inward, toward itself, creating an enveloping experience and allowing your gaze to penetrate the veil between the worlds.

Convex Mirrors

A convex mirror pushes light, images, and energy outward at a greater rate than a flat mirror. Its reflective surface is bent to expand the view, light, and therefore energy. Examples of these kinds of curved mirrors are the mirrors sometimes used at the end of a driveway to see traffic if it's on a dangerous intersection; also, you sometimes see them in shops because with a wider view, they help with security. If there's a mirror on your car that has the label "objects in the mirror are closer than they appear," then that mirror is slightly convex so that you can get a wider view of the road, but it makes the cars look like they are a little farther away than they actually are. Some trucks have a round and even more convex mirror attached to the side mirror to help them get a wider view so they can see behind them and avoid accidents.

Knowing convex mirrors' everyday use might point to their magical use. A silver convex mirror is a wonderful tool for deflecting negative energies. Think of the shape of it: it's like a shiny shield for deflecting metaphysical arrows. My favorite type of convex witch's mirror is the *oeil de sorcière* (sorcerer's eye or witch's eye). These are lovely decorative pieces that are great for halting hexes, negative magic, or harmful energy of any kind in its tracks. It also represents an eye, but not just any eye: the reflective eye of a higher power or deity looking out for you. This kind of mirror can act as a warning, offering magical awareness of your surroundings and the incoming energies. It's a magical security system that, depending on your intentions, either reverses or returns attacks from whence they came or sends them into the universe to be neutralized. The convex mirror is a great choice for a magical mirror to watch over your finances; after all, they were sometimes called "banker's eye" due to their security uses, as they keep an eye on your fortune, in addition to having been originally considered status symbols.

I have seen a few black scrying mirrors that are convex, although traditionally most curved black mirrors tend to be concave. The reason for this is that a convex mirror tends to reflect more of the room around you, so it may cause distraction. That being said, many people love scrying in a crystal or even obsidian sphere with an outwardly curving surface, so if you prefer, you can certainly use a convex black scrying mirror, but before you do, consider the magical purposes of the shapes of mirrors.

MIRROR LORE
Never hang a mirror so that the reflection cuts the top of your head off or you'll get headaches.

Bagua Mirror

Bagua mirrors are little mirrors used in feng shui that pack a powerful punch. While octagon-shaped and curved witch's mirrors are fine to enchant and use inside the home, bagua mirrors specifically made for feng shui are strictly for outdoor

Which Mirrors for Witch's Mirrors?

use. A bagua mirror is usually a round mirror set within an octagon-shaped frame with special symbols all around it, and it doesn't know how to use its inside voice. In feng shui the energies that convex baguas are meant to cure are called either "poison arrow" or "shar" energy, which refers to harmful energies such as those that might emanate from nightmare neighbors, a busy road, or inauspicious building nearby. Concave bagua mirrors can be used to draw in energy from positive, uplifting views or neutralize passively negative energy such as a badly placed tree.

These very specific kinds of mirrors are meant only for use outside the home, unless prescribed by a feng shui expert. They are energy powerhouses; using one of these inside your home would be like spraying industrial outdoor insecticide in your kitchen because you saw an ant! (Really! Just don't do it.) You can also cause more harm than good if you use the wrong bagua mirror in the wrong placement; feng shui is pretty complex. Consult a good feng shui book—or, better yet, an expert—before deciding on the placement of a bagua mirror, just to be sure.

My Favorite Mirror

One of the most magical mirrors in my life is a concave mirror inside a telescope that is roughly the size of a small hot-water heater. Remember when those two astronomers discovered

Comet Hale-Bopp in 1995? Well, if you're as geeky as I am, you might; welcome to the club! I'm talking about a telescope much like the ones they used to see that comet two years before it was visible in our skies.

That mirror—my favorite magic mirror in the whole world—was hand-ground by my grandfather, who in his day was one of the most sought-after craftsman of telescope mirrors in the country. Mirrors he crafted reflect the heavens through telescopes in every county in the US, and he once even received a request from NASA.

Grandpa was also a Freemason of a high degree; having a mystical side as well, I suspect that when he looked through his telescopes he saw more than floating rocks and burning gasses in space. It's likely he imagined the deeper mysteries of the universe reflected in that mirror.

When I look through the telescope he built that my mother, sister, and I inherited from him, I can see the rings of Saturn, Venus herself, and the spiraling masses of distant galaxies, and I also can see the spirit of my grandfather. That mirror is a perfect example of the dichotomy of the magic mirror: it looks both inward and outward, infinitely. Now I use very different methods than he did to make and use mirrors for witchcraft, but I still love using his mirror to see the universe. I think he would smile at the thought of my witchy mirrors.

Everyday Mirrors Are Magic Too

You probably have tons of mirrors all over your home. What about the mirror over your bathroom sink, the big mirror behind the dining room table, or the compact mirror in your purse—can those be witch's mirrors? You bet they can! Mirrors are really pretty common items; in today's world you can get a simple mirror for magical use pretty much anywhere. The household mirrors that we all own are generally made of glass with aluminum on the back.

Aluminum may not seem very magical since we use it to cover leftover meatloaf or drink canned soft drinks out of, but it's a very magical metal. The most abundant metal on earth, aluminum is a metal traditionally used for magical psychic protection and travel magic, and it is believed to boost mental abilities. Aluminum is associated with the planet Mercury. It's an element that reflects and repels any unwanted energies, creating great magical protection. Aluminum also balances body energies. Knowing that, the household mirror suddenly seems much more magical, doesn't it?

As an example of the power of aluminum and a few makeshift witch's mirrors, here's a story. Once when I was involved with a coven, one of our members had a neighbor who had a bad habit of leering at her over the fence and being a general creepy nuisance; she felt uncomfortable in her own backyard. We were at her house for a coven gathering when she mentioned it, and we all decided something must be done right there on the spot. After the initial jokes about calling out our flying monkeys or giving him a pentagram-shaped rash, it was decided that some impromptu mirror magic was in order. The best thing she had on hand were a few miniature aluminum pie pans. Perfect! We all put our heads together and whipped up a quick spell to enchant the pie pans to bounce those creepy vibes back over the fence where they belonged—only what he sent, with no harm to him intended.

Did it work? After the first week, she reported that he suddenly quit his lurking behavior and she noticed that the backyard felt much safer and more comfortable. Whatever intentions he was sending over that fence must not have been good because when they were being reflected back at him, it was enough to keep his attention on his own side of the fence. Those were simply aluminum pie pans until our coven of protective witches got our hands on them.

Can you enchant a regular old household mirror for your magical purpose? You absolutely can. A mirror that's an antique, purchased from any shop, or one that already exists in your home also can become a witch's mirror.

The Scoop on Mirror Washes and Fluid Condensers

This is a topic that could make your head spin if you let it, but I've done the research so you don't have to. Here's the no-nonsense lowdown on charging a witch's mirror by using either a mirror wash or the seemingly elusive and sometimes confusing formula known as a fluid condenser. For our purposes, both are made using infusions, which is very much like a tea: simply put herbs in boiled water. But there are differences in the two (don't worry—I'll explain).

A mirror wash is a magical infusion of herbs that have been steeped in hot water. Generally, leaves and flowers can be placed into a jar or cup and you can pour boiling water over them, allowing them to steep, much like a tea. If you have roots or bark you may prefer to actually boil them in the water for a few minutes, since they're tougher, in order to release the essence of the plant into the water. Either way, you strain it after it's cool. I like to mix mine with vinegar, but lots of witches make washes of just herbs and water that work wonderfully. I personally like to add the vinegar because the combination of water and vinegar is the perfect substance for cleaning all kinds of glass, so my mirrors are both empowered and smudge free—ever the kitchen witch, I guess!

When you use a mirror wash, you apply the infusion of those herbs directly onto your mirror, and the vibrations of the herbs can adjust the vibrations of the mirror and help program it to your specific magical purpose. The herbs can be added to boiling water, like a tea, and then strained, leaving that lovely herby magic in the liquid; if you wish, add vinegar after the infusion cools. Mirror washes can be stored in pretty wine bottles or even plastic or glass spray bottles. It is then applied to the mirror's front or back in the same way that you would wash a mirror: apply the liquid and rub it in with a soft cloth or paper towel while repeating a magical charm to activate it. You can also include a few drops of gem elixirs as part of a mirror wash. A mirror wash is pretty easy to make, requires very few special skills, and most of the ingredients are readily available.

Fluid condensers are another way to magically charge a mirror that we especially see used for black scrying mirrors but could be used for silver mirrors as well. A fluid condenser is a little fancier than a wash and usually includes more exotic ingredients such as gold, silver, and sometimes bodily fluids of the person who created it. Condensers are a bit more challenging to make. They are usually made from infusions that are boiled and then strained and boiled again to reduce and concentrate the liquid. Then the mixture is added to some kind of clear alcohol such as vodka.

What's all the fuss about fluid condensers? Part of what people find hard to wrap their heads around is the name—*fluid condenser*—which doesn't mean what it sounds like it means. Fluid condensers don't have to be in the form of a liquid, but they often are. Just to add to the confusion, there are also solid fluid condensers that are actually powders but are still referred to as fluid condensers, thus leading to befuddlement and hair pulling by many of us modern witches. Is it fluid? Is it solid? What?!

Which Mirrors for Witch's Mirrors?

Don't worry—I did some digging and I'm here to clarify, once and for all, what it all means. The term "fluid" in this context *doesn't* mean liquid; it actually refers to magical and spiritual energy and power that "flows like fluid" between the everyday world and the spiritual realm. The term "condenser" describes the process of condensing the liquid, as well as the fact that it's also an old term from the 1800s used to describe what we now call a capacitor, which basically stores energy. Occultists from Victorian times often compared electrical and magnetic energy with spiritual energy in their writings, so it makes sense that they would call this special kind of application a fluid condenser because it's a mixture that acts as a capacitor, storing spirit or aether energy. (Aha!)

In the 1800s Paschal Beverly Randolph used fluid condensers for his famous magic mirrors, and those ideas were very successfully expanded upon later by Franz Bardon in the 1950s. Bardon published some very accessible works on the subject and included instructions for making and working with fluid condensers for mirrors and other purposes. Many occultists since have created formulas for condensers. Simple fluid condensers can be made of just one plant and metal tincture; some people add a drop of blood or other bodily fluids, but only if the condenser will be used by the person who made it. A popular multipurpose condenser is made with chamomile, as described by both Franz Bardon and Sybil Leek. They also both published formulas for specific elemental energies of earth, air, fire, water, and akasha (spirit), as well as condensers charged with planetary energy. The basic method is to boil equal parts of plant material and water for thirty minutes, cool, filter, and then boil again to concentrate the liquid. Some formulas add alcohol once it's cooled. If you try the ones I've included in this book and want to make more, I highly recommend the book *Initiation Into Hermetics* by Franz Bardon for great classic formulas for fluid condensers.

To sum up: *mirror washes* are liquid herbal infusions boiled or steeped once and used alone or mixed with vinegar. Mirror washes are generally magically charged with a specific purpose, such as love, prosperity, healing, or protection. *Fluid condensers* are herbal infusions boiled twice and sometimes mixed with alcohol, and they may include metals or exotic ingredients. Fluid condensers can also be in forms that are not liquid, such as powders or vapors. Fluid condensers are usually aligned magically with planets or elemental powers such as Venus, Mars, air, fire, water, or earth rather than specific magical intentions.

Which is better for enchanting your witch's mirror, condensers or washes? It's really all about the energy you, as a witch, put into it. What's your style? As far as the two methods, it's a matter of whichever one is your magical cup of tea. Take a look at the formulas for both in chapter 7; you might even like to experiment with both washes and condensers.

Which Mirrors for Witch's Mirrors?

Frames, Stands, and Hangers

Some mirrors need to be in frames; it's the best way to display a mirror on the wall in your home or office. If you have a mirror that needs a frame, there are many options. Some people prefer something brand-new from a department store or specialty frame shop where you can find any style you like. As an artist I happen to know brand-new frames and professional framing can be pretty pricey, but if you have the resources, go for it. If you're on a tighter budget, though, there are many good frames of all shapes and sizes to be found in secondhand stores. I once had a one-woman show in a local gallery with my art in discount frames that I painted so they would all match. I'm a witchy artist with an eye for a bargain, so I'm not above looking in unusual places for magical supplies.

Don't limit yourself to empty frames while thrifting, either; most of the framed art you'll find at secondhand stores are just low-quality commercial prints that you can toss without remorse and keep the frame for your mirror. Look for frames that can be easily opened from the back and resealed; also be sure it's made using quality construction. Look for real wood and metal, and steer clear from plastic frames, which can break easily and put your mirror at risk. The key to thrifting a frame for your witch's mirror—or any magical tool, for that matter—is to carefully clean it first physically, then cleanse any vibes from the previous owner or that ugly orange-and-purple flower print that was in it. Do this by using an herbal wash (such as the new mirror purifier in chapter 7), sprinkling it with salt or herbs, passing it through smudge stick or incense smoke, or doing a combination of these techniques. I find an antique frame for a witch's mirror to be positively charming.

It's important to make sure you hang your framed mirror securely. If it's heavy, be sure to find a wall stud to put your nail into. You can also use one of those super strong Hercules Hooks or any of the other brands of similar hooks to make sure your mirror doesn't fall and break.

If you need to add a hanger to the back of the frame, I strongly recommend using two small eye hooks and gallery wire (yep, I grew up in art galleries). You can pick up both of these items at the hardware store, and they're very strong and easy to use. Measure down from the top of the frame about one-third of the length down; the eye hooks just screw into the back of the frame, a little bit in from the edge. Cut the gallery wire longer than you think you need and run it through both eye hooks, making sure that the middle of the wire, when pulled up to the top of the frame, will come about an inch or two below the top of the frame. Just twist the end of the wire around itself tightly like a twist tie for bread. You can add a bit of masking tape to the wire ends so they don't scratch your wall.

Which Mirrors for Witch's Mirrors?

For some kinds of witch's mirrors, you might prefer some kind of a stand. Small tabletop easels found in craft stores work great. They come in all kinds of materials—metal, wood, even resin. These easels are very useful for scrying mirrors and can be just the thing for propping up a mirror on a table, altar, or other workspace so that you can sit comfortably while attempting to scry. If you find an easel you want to use, you can always add your own touch to make it magical: use paint, attach beads or charms with wire, burn magical designs in wood—let your imagination run wild.

Some kinds of mirrored items to be used for magic can be displayed on hangers. You can hang a mirrored ball, ornament, or suncatcher in a window using a hook over the window or a suction cup. Another great way to display a witch's mirrored item or ornament that can be hung is by using a wire ornament stand—the kind you find during the holidays for displaying special ornaments. The nice thing about these stands is that you can then place a hanging mirrored item anywhere you please. I once lucked out and found a round, flat piece of glass with a hole at the top that was meant to be turned into a suncatcher. I made it into a black scrying mirror and hung it from a brass wire ornament hanger. Always be on the lookout; you never know what you'll find!

· · ·
Chapter 3

Useful Tips: How to Store, Protect, and Recharge Your Witch's Mirror

Some mirrors will be kept on the wall, keeping a watchful eye, filling your home with blessings, or reminding you of your beautiful and amazing inner witch. Mirrors in frames that you intend to keep out need only to be hung securely in order to protect them.

There are some witch's mirrors, however, that you only bring out for occasional use. These mirrors are obviously going to need to have some kind of protection while they're not in use. Many people prefer to keep scrying mirrors out of the sunlight; at the very least, it's smart to keep your mirrors protected from scratches or breaking, gods forbid! Boxes, satin or velvet bags, or even a fancy scarf can help you protect your magic mirror when not in use.

If you have a box that your mirror will fit in, consider lining the box with some thick quilt batting covered with velvet or satin to keep it from getting banged around in the box. You can use a wooden box if you like, or even one of those fancy decorative chipboard boxes we see in all the craft stores. If you don't want to go to all the trouble of adding a liner or it won't work well for the box you have, you can fill the box with shredded paper and sandwich it in between. If you must, bubble wrap is a perfectly good choice; the kind with the gigantic bubbles the size of a half dollar works best for flat breakables. My husband, Dan, and I package and ship breakables all over the world. When using regular packing supplies such as paper or bubble wrap, I like to put the mirror in a drawstring bag or wrap it in a silk scarf or some other nice fabric first, then use packing supplies; this keeps the mirror sacred and not in direct contact with your packaging.

Another thing you might consider making room for in the box is a tightly sealed bottle of your specific herb wash or condenser if you've made one for that particular mirror. Then if you feel it needs to be recharged, you don't have to go digging around—you'll have it right at your fingertips. The best time to recharge your mirror is during the same part of the lunar cycle as when you first charged it. Try to store liquids upright; if that's not an option, seal the bottle in a no-leak zipper bag for safety.

MIRROR LORE

*If you have to return home because
you forgot something, before you leave
the house again, make a face or stick
out your tongue in a mirror to frighten
away any evil spirits on the other side.*

My Personal Experience with Mirrors and Magic

For scrying, I have found that a darker surface works better for me—I have even used an unlit iPad in a pinch! Just use a bit of vinegar in water and carefully wipe the surface before using with a candle for light in a darkened room. However, for a deeper session, whether alone or in a group, I prefer to have a 9-inch round dark scrying mirror that is kept in a dark bag and only has seen moonlight and candlelight since it was consecrated for scrying use only. I had a friend make one for me years ago that I still use (she used black felt and round clear glass loaded with intention, and even made astrological glyphs for me alone). People who have better clairvoyant skills do much better with my mirror than even I do—they are usually dominant in the water element. Since I am an astrologer, I actually tune in on symbols and really "know" messages better than actually seeing people or what will happen (called claircognizance), and if I need timing, I then reach for my pendulum, as dowsing is more of my natural gift than mirror work.

That being said, I have used mirrors in spellwork in three ways: to either repel or send back energy, to magnify results, and to create a shield or an illusion that is usually put in place for protection more than anything else. In the 1990s when I had very little money, the computer stores always had AOL or Earthlink disks for free to access dial-up Internet. Those CDs were perfect to use! After I cleaned them, I even programmed a use for the hole in the middle, which was to allow the good, pure, loving light energies into whatever work I was doing.

Spirits like to hide in all things shiny, especially smooth surfaces, so mirrors are their first choice, and they use them as portals for travel to other dimensions too. To cut the psychic/astral "chatter" and close inappropriate portals, I clean all mirrors, windows, and shiny surfaces with a dampened cloth in vinegar water (1 tablespoon any kind of vinegar to 16 ounces water, distilled or spring is best; a pinch of salt will help also) and clean with the intention of clearing the portals I wish to close or eliminate; if done well, you won't have to repeat that too often. Holy water, cascaria, or smudging with white desert sage or palo santo helps too. Adding flower essences to the cleansing water can also help. I have friends who use essential oils with menthol on cotton balls (camphor, mints, eucalyptus, etc.) or even cut an onion and place a piece in each corner to absorb negativity (mulch the onion after a day or two). You may create a boundary for the contact(s) you *do* want when you are ready by then using mugwort leaves, making a strong tea or tincture in water to wipe onto the mirror, as well as your third eye; take some internally (without sweetener is best) to further enhance your vision. There are other dreaming and vision herbs, but mugwort is usually most accessible and best. You may have access to moxa sticks to use as smudge, which is how acupuncturists use mugwort.

Happy scrying!

Calantirniel
Professional author, astrologer, herbalist, tarot card reader, dowser, energy healer, ULC reverend, flower essence creator/ practitioner, and co-founder of Tië eldaliéva • www.AstroHerbalist.com, www.ElvenSpirituality.com

chapter
4

Mirror, Mirror
on the Go

Now that you know you always have magical mirrors all around you, let's look at some magic you can make with them on the fly. As we've learned, all mirrors are full of the power to reflect or absorb energy; that's why so many superstitions revolve around everyday mirrors, not just especially enchanted and magically charged ones.

Here are some quickie spells you can work using everyday mirrors without any kind of special mirror preparation. For these little spells, you can create some powerful magic in a flash just by using the mirror's natural magical properties! Maybe these quick and easy spells will inspire some of your own magic that you can make with any mirror, anywhere, anytime!

"Reflective Specs" Psychic Shield

I know lots of people who are introverts and do not like being in big crowds of people. Many people love the excitement of a festival, parade, or big, bustling mall, but for people who have social anxiety, are empathic, or are even just not in the mood, it can become very overwhelming. If you find yourself in a situation where you're at a big event and it's just too much, here's a quick way to create a psychic shield until you feel ready to handle it.

Keep a pair of mirrored sunglasses handy. The more the pair you choose goes with your style, the better; look for something cool that makes a statement—then you look like you're going with the flow instead of hiding out. If things just get to be too much, pop the mirrored shades on and visualize the reflecting surface radiating out from the glasses to envelop your entire body. As you do, repeat an affirmation inside your head for just a minute or so; try something like:

> *Quiet, calm, and cool*
> *Mellow as a mirrored pool*

You can peer over the tops of the glasses little by little until you feel adjusted with the energy of the event. Leave them on as long as you need to.

Compact Mirror Wishing Spell

For this spell, any compact mirror will do—and when the spell is complete, it can still be used to touch up your lipstick. What's a dream, wish, or miracle you're hoping for? You know—that wish you might make upon a star? Do you wish to find true love? Move up in the world? Get healthy? Find a way to earn seed money for a new business? While you're trying to make that wish come true by everyday means, why not help it along with a little mirror magic?

You'll need a compact mirror with two mirrors face to face when you close it. Most of those kinds of compacts have one flat mirror and one concave mirror (the magnifying mirror is the concave one). Gaze into your own eye reflected in the magnifying side and recite the charm to activate the mirror:

> *Mirror, mirror, a wish I ask*
> *Manifest it as your task*
> *Take it to the other side*
> *My wish comes true you'll gently guide*

Now whisper your wish into the eye of your own reflection, followed by "with harm to none, so mote it be." Close the compact and allow your reflection to take your wish to the otherworld and make it manifest. Don't forget that magick follows the path of least resistance, so find a few things to do in the real world to help your wish along. May your wishes come true!

Mirror, Mirror on the Go

"Put It Behind You" Rearview Mirror Spell

This spell should be done during the daytime only—Saturday is a good day—and during a waning or a dark moon. Letting go of something that's bugging you can be a challenge; you know, the stuff that dances through your head and makes you feel bad about yourself. Some people call it negative self-talk. That can really put a damper on things for you in life, so here's a quick mirror spell to cast away those thoughts that keep sabotaging your success.

First, identify the thought you keep saying to yourself that's holding you back. Does a phrase like "I never do anything right" or "I'll never get ahead" ever pop into your head? Whatever it is, first identify it and write it down using a fine pointed permanent marker on a large leaf (I suggest, elder, oak, or poplar). Get into your car and drive to a place you don't usually go, someplace like a park or a commuter parking lot, and make sure it's a safe place. Back into a parking space and park. Look at the leaf and repeat the negative message that keeps repeating in your head aloud; this shines the light of day on it. Hold the words up to the rearview mirror of your car so that you can see the words reflected backwards, then say, "I reverse this negative thought; it no longer has a place in my heart." Get out of the car and look around for a rock big enough to see in your rearview mirror when you're sitting in your car. Place it behind your car, within view of your rearview mirror, and put the leaf beneath it, then say firmly, "I don't want you anymore." Now get in your car, look through your rearview mirror at the rock with the leaf beneath it, and repeat this charm three times:

> *I release this phrase from my heart and soul*
> *I do not hear you anymore*
> *You're in my past and there you'll stay*
> *I won't miss you a bit as I drive away*

Do not turn around; only look at it through the rearview mirror—a magic mirror meant to see only things that are behind you. Start your car and drive away. As you pull up in your driveway, sit there for a moment knowing that negative phrase you were telling yourself is gone, but remember nature abhors a vacuum. The final and most important step of this spell needs to happen now. Look into your own eyes in the rearview mirror and tell yourself the phrase you will replace the negative one with. Say it eighteen times. For instance, "I'm capable of doing anything I decide to do" or "I can go as far in my life as I choose." Anytime that old phrase tries to pop into your head, replace it immediately with your new phrase. As the leaf under the rock that you left behind decomposes, so will the negative statement disappear and be completely replaced with the positive.

Mirror, Mirror on the Go

Quick Office Feng Shui

If things aren't quite flowing well in your work or home office, there are a few feng shui strategies you can apply using simple mirrors to brighten your environment and keep your positive chi flowing. If your back is to the door and you can't move your desk, try placing a mirror so that you can see the door from your desk. This will help you have more control over your environment, putting you in a power position and keeping you feeling stable at your desk.

Deflecting negative energy of a problematic coworker is easy to do using a small, unobtrusive mirror. Even a tiny craft mirror can work. You can put it behind something so that it's not even seen; attach it to your cubicle and put a soothing picture over the top of it if you want. As long as you aim it in the direction of the offending or aggressive person, even if they're on the other side of the wall, it will work if you do it with intention.

When you place the mirror, be sure that you do it with no harmful intentions to them (I know, but trust me on this…). Just use the intention that they keep any drama, insults, or gossip regarding you to themselves. Using a mirror in this way asserts that the other person's problems are their own, and you are leaving them to deal with it on their own without involving you. Usually the situation will ramp down considerably, and they may even end up with a transfer to a position more suitable to their temperament—then everyone is happier!

When placing mirrors for feng shui, try using a hand gesture, focusing on your intention and a mantra to reinforce your mirror. First, use the Karana mudra, a sacred hand gesture where your index and pinkie finger point up, middle and ring fingers are bent down together, and the thumb rests on the fingertip of the middle finger. This mudra expels evil. While using this hand gesture, focus on your intention and purpose for the mirror you are placing. Now use a sacred mantra nine times. (If you need to, whisper this while everyone is on their lunch break or come in early that day.) I like the "six true words" mantra: *om ma ni pad me hum*, which, translated loosely, means "I bow to the jewel of the lotus/inner self." Now you've done more than hang a mirror; you've created sacred magic.

MIRROR LORE
A large mirror under your bed
facing up is a cure for insomnia.

Store Window Looking Glass Spell

This spell on the go was inspired by a story about my mother's childhood. When my mom was a kid, everyone got dressed up to go shopping, and an outing to the shopping district was quite a big deal. She used to love seeing her reflection mingled with all of the beautiful items on display in the windows of the department stores and visualized herself in a different world where the store displays were part of her life. To her those windows were magical mirrors.

When you're out shopping at the mall, the local shopping district, or favorite city street, keep your eyes open for a window display that represents something you want to manifest in your life. If you need a vacation, look for a travel agency or exotic importer. Are you seeking knowledge or college scholarships? Try your local bookseller. Do you want to fill your life with all the shoes? Well, you get the idea. Are you ready to surround yourself with beauty and abundance? Let's go shopping!

Upon finding your window display of choice, walk back and forth a bit until you find your reflection superimposed with a perfect representation of what you want to manifest. Focus on the combination of your reflection and the display. Now, you're in public, so you'll be thinking this, not saying it aloud, but you need to tell your reflection what you want. Try something like, "My reflection knows what I wish to hold."

Repeat it several times until you feel the spell is cast, and right before you walk away, say, "As I will, with harm to none, so mote it be."

Anywhere Quick Mirror Glamoury

This is a quick mirror meditation to fill your aura with positive energy, letting your inner beauty shine through. Say you're having a bad hair day, you're not looking your best, or you're just feeling tired, and you suddenly find yourself in a situation where you really need some fast glamoury. Find a mirror, any mirror—it can be a compact, bathroom mirror, even a dressing room mirror. Smooth yourself down the best you can.

Now, looking into the mirror, visualize how you want to be perceived projected over your reflection as you let a golden light begin to build in your solar plexus, located about an inch higher than your belly button. See yourself how you want to appear. Focus on that image of confidence as you let that golden light swirl, grow, and begin to fill your whole body.

Allow the golden light to extend out to your aura, surrounding you with the light, and fill that light with the image of yourself looking your best, confidant, full of magic, programming the light with that image. Once you feel it's fully in place, you're good to go. Stand proud, tall, and get out there. Face the world, knowing that your mirror magic glamoury won't actually change how you look, but it will influence how others perceive you.

"Chill Out" Kaleidoscope Spell

Stress—it can really wreck your day. Have you just had too much on your mind lately? You need a way to clear your head and focus on something else for long enough to awaken your deep-down happiness and release that stress.

A mirror from your childhood—well, actually, three very magical mirrors—is the key. Those kaleidoscopes we all played with as kids made their beautiful images by reflecting little bits of plastic in three mirrors that formed an equilateral triangle. There are all kinds of kaleidoscopes, from fancy high-end stained glass or wooden ones filled with genuine stones or glass to simple ones made of plastic and cardboard from the dollar store. For this spell, you can use any kind. If you're really handy, you might like to take apart one of the cheap dollar store ones, redecorate it, and replace the plastic beads and bits with small tumbled stones, tiny crystal points, silver charms, or fancy glass beads, the smaller the better. You don't have to do this, though; it will work just fine as is.

No matter what kind of kaleidoscope you have, take it outside and lie down if weather and space permit. If you can't get outside, just lie down on the floor anyplace where you have a nice light to comfortably aim it at. Spend a little time looking through it, turning the tumbler and seeing what kinds of shapes and colors come up. I bet you haven't played with a kaleidoscope in ages!

Now that you've refamiliarized yourself with the optical wonder again, move it away from your eye, shake it up, and then, holding it in your hands, imagine all the stress you've been feeling pouring into the kaleidoscope. Now take a deep breath in through your nose and release it out through your mouth as you hold the kaleidoscope up to your eye and observe the peaceful colors. Begin to turn the tumbler in a counterclockwise direction slowly and repeat a simple mantra such as "release" over and over, but slowly, peacefully. Allow the beauty of the patterns to unfold as the stress you've been feeling is drawn through the patterns and up. Patterns are created and then break apart, creating new patterns; as each pattern breaks, more stress is released. Allow everything to release upward, spiraling and transforming; the mirrors bounce the energy up toward the pattern they reflect and the turning of the tumbler draws it up and out toward the light. As you turn the tumbler, you should feel lighter and lighter, with the weight of stress being lifted.

Once you're done, you should be able to approach the situation that brought on the stress with a new, peaceful frame of mind, which makes figuring out a good course of action for problem-solving a much smoother and easier task.

Mirror, Mirror on the Go

Bonus Spell: Kaleidoscope Divination

Do you still have that kaleidoscope from the last spell? Remember, it's made out of three mirrors that create random images. Why not use a kaleidoscope for divination in the same way you would read tea leaves in a cup?

Hold the kaleidoscope in your hands and ask a question that you want more insight about. Put the kaleidoscope up to your eye and turn clockwise while you repeat the following charm three times:

Color and light
Bring me insight

Then stop and keep the tumbler still; the pattern now revealed should offer suggestions to your answers. Look for shapes you recognize in the pattern—a horseshoe for luck, a butterfly for transformation or rebirth, a crown for successfully achieving your goals. Watch for patterns in the light as well as in the patterns themselves. You can also analyze your answer based on the colors that are most prominent and those that are less prominent. Check out the appendices at the back of this book for meanings of some of the color themes and symbols you might find.

Melanie Marquis

Moon Mirror
Lucky Charm

As a witch, I usually prefer to let Nature take her own course, but every now and then, circumstances arise that prompt me to take a bit of swift and decisive magickal action. Whenever you feel that fate needs a little nudge in the right direction, try this simple mirror charm that makes use not only of the mirror's inherent attributes, but also utilizes powerful lunar energies to weave your spell.

You'll need a compact mirror with a lid that closes, like the kind that face powder typically comes in. On the night of the full moon, take the mirror outside and think of your wish. If you like, choose something small to represent that wish, like a drop of essential oil or a piece of dried herb that has energies corresponding to your intentions, or a scrap of paper on which you've written your desire or drawn a glyph that symbolizes your magickal goal.

With your intention clearly in mind, look up at the moon in the sky, then open the mirror so that the moon's image is reflected on the glassy surface. See how the moonlight streams down all the way from the heavens to show its face to the mirror. Look at the moon's reflection and express your wish. You might choose to follow up with the verse:

> *Light, luck, and lunar powers*
> *Open doors and blooming flowers*
> *The moon shares her light with me*
> *And what I want will surely be*

If you've chosen an object to represent your wish, place it on the moon's reflection and close the mirror; if you're not using any extra ingredients, simply close the mirror without delay, taking a final look at the moon's reflection as the lid of the compact closes.

The mirror is now enchanted to act as a magickal charm to help you achieve your goals and attract what you desire. Carry the mirror with you and keep it in the closed position. Whenever you find yourself daydreaming about the success you wish to achieve, take out the mirror, open it briefly, smile at your reflection, and say to yourself, "I'll get it!" Then close the mirror and put it back in its usual place.

The charm will last for roughly one month. Recharge at the next full moon.

Melanie Marquis
Author of *A Witch's World of Magick*
and *The Witch's Bag of Tricks* •
www.melaniemarquis.com

chapter
5

Finding a Mirror to Reflect Your Witchy Style

Everyday mirrors are great to work with magically, but now that we've talked about all these different kinds of mirrors, you may want to try out a special magically enchanted witch's mirror. Here, I'll share my shopping tips on where you can find some of these magical, mystical mirrors. Would you just love a concave scrying mirror of your very own, Hexenspiegel jewelry to wear everywhere, or an Old World *oeil de sorcière* to watch over you? I have fallen in love with these mysterious witch's tools, and I'm excited to tell you that they are easier to get your witchy fingers on than you might think.

Magic Mirrors: Shall We Shop?

Come window shopping with me—I know all the good places, no matter your budget. Let's look at where to begin the search for your very own witch's mirror.

Some kinds of magical mirrors are easier to just purchase unless you have special skills, tools, and supplies. Perhaps you are the kind of witch who finds something that's almost perfect and tweaks it yourself. Many crafty witches would rather make their own and just need to know where to find the supplies.

Just like any other magical tool, no matter where you get your mirror, it's important to cleanse any residual energy from it before consecrating it for a magical purpose. This step is very important for mirrors since they literally carry other people's reflections and energies within them. You don't know whose reflection may have been in the mirror before you got ahold of it, no matter where it came from. Even if the mirror has been in your own home for awhile, it's best to do a cleansing on it before you enchant it to remove any negative vibes from family arguments, snippy guests, or bad hair days.

I like to clean my everyday mirrors or new mirrors I intend to use for magic with a vinegar and water purifier. This goes back to my days growing up among the who's who of artists on the scene in Albuquerque, New Mexico, and being there while they were hanging my dad's watercolors in art galleries all over the Southwest. Paintings behind glass were all hung carefully and then the last of the fingerprints were wiped off using newspaper and spray bottles filled with water and vinegar, leaving them sparkly clean for the art show opening. Your mirror is art too—it reflects the art of your life, the scenes of love and beauty, and also the art of your powerful and unique magic. A magic mirror deserves respect, so instead of chemical cleaners, a simple water and vinegar mixture creates a good magical base for physical and energetic cleaning and respects everything that it reflects. The formula for my magical new mirror purifier is in chapter 7; I recommend it for cleaning all your new magic mirrors before you start working with them.

MIRROR LORE
There is an old belief that it's unlucky for the sick to see their reflections; their soul, being more vulnerable, might become trapped.

Finding a Mirror to Reflect Your Witchy Style

Seeking Out a Black Scrying Mirror

A black mirror—the classic scrying tool for divination, astral travel, otherworldly communication, and more—is traditionally made of onyx, obsidian, or glass. While most mirrors are designed to be highly reflective and portray an accurate image of the world we live in, a black mirror is meant to create a deep pure black surface for your eyes to focus on while viewing other worlds. You can find obsidian scrying mirrors, sometimes called a "shew stone," online (*shew* is an antiquated spelling of *show*); you could also check your local metaphysical shop to see if they carry them if you want to go really old-school. You need special equipment to grind and smooth a large flat or concave piece of onyx or obsidian; most people would just find one to purchase.

Some people like to use a one- or two-inch black onyx or obsidian pendant as a scrying mirror. I have a terrible time scrying in something as small as a pendant, but lots of people have great success with them. I get too distracted by my peripheral vision. Peripheral vision is the area beyond the 3 percent area we can focus our eyes on at one time. Test your peripheral vision by standing with your back against a wall and arms outstretched like a cross on either side. While staring at a fixed point straight ahead, wiggle your fingers as you slowly move your arms away from the wall. If you get distracted and are tempted to look at your fingers when they are a foot or less away from the wall, you might benefit from a larger-sized mirror for scrying rather than a small item like a pendant.

You can also find many varieties of black glass scrying mirrors in local shops and online; they come in many sizes and are usually square or round. They also vary from flat to concave. Although I have seen a few convex black mirrors, both a flat or concave shape are traditional. The concave shape helps keep distracting light off of the surface since it curves in like a bowl, and it also energetically draws your eye and third eye inward. With these mirrors, the black is always on the back, or convex side, of the mirror, so that your viewing area (the concave side) is a sheet of glass with black behind it; this is important because it adds depth to the surface.

These mirrors are not hard to make yourself; in fact, creating your own black scrying mirror can be a really rewarding experience. All you really need is a piece of concave or flat clear glass and some black enamel paint. You can add magical condensers, washes, special frames, magical symbols, and stones to suit your needs; it can be as streamlined or as fancy as you like.

Dahling, That Hexenspiegel Looks Divine on You!

Hexenspiegel means "witch's mirror" in German. It's usually a mirrored pendant, bracelet, or other kind of small mirrored item that is enchanted magically and worn. Hexenspiegels

Finding a Mirror to Reflect Your Witchy Style

can also be carried in a pocket or purse, or they can be displayed in the home to shield the user from the evil eye and all forms of negative energy. What differentiates a Hexenspiegel from other witch's mirrors is they are generally small and are enchanted for a specific purpose, using herbs of the old Germanic witch's cupboard and your intention to refuse to accept astral nasties sent your way. It's generally a preventative that you can put in place or wear to prevent intrusive or harmful magic, the evil eye, or hateful intentions. The other thing that sets Hexenspiegel magic apart is that it not only repels harm, but it sends any negative energy sent to you right back to the attacker, so this is a little tiny mirror with some pretty serious magic.

Think of it like this: if a person offers you a gift and you decline, the ownership of that gift remains with the giver. The same is true with baneful energy; the Hexenspiegel does set off warning bells to attackers, and if they don't heed the warning, it simply says, "Thanks, but no thanks," letting any sender of ill intentions remain the owner of their own nasty gift. The Hexenspiegel is an automatic kind of magic—create it, place it, and forget it; it keeps on doing its job without any further attention from you.

There are a few online sellers that sell pre-enchanted Hexenspiegels, but they're not always easy to find; fortunately, with the right spell any small silver-type mirror can be enchanted and turned into a Hexenspiegel. Mirrored pendants became popular in Victorian times, and today you can find both actual antiques and reproductions of fancy decorative mirror pendants in many styles, from decorative to modern, at many price ranges. If you can't find mirror jewelry locally, just try a quick search online; there are many out there.

Some mirror pendants are inside a locket or are otherwise hidden; yes, they do still work even if covered. Keeping this in mind, another great mirror to make into a Hexenspiegel is a small compact mirror you can keep in your purse; with a little luck, you might even find one with a magical symbol on it. There are also small mirrors meant for men to keep in their wallets that can be enchanted as a Hexenspiegel, so if you prefer not to wear a mirror, carrying one will work just as well. Remember, it's the enchantment you place on it that transforms it from a regular small mirror into a Hexenspiegel that constantly refuses and returns bad vibes to their sender.

You can also find small mirror jewelry components at your local craft store, so you could make a necklace, earrings, or even a charm bracelet in your own style. Include stones for magical protection to boost your Hexenspiegel, such as moonstone, tiger's eye, black tourmaline, or labradorite. You could even add special charms, such as your totem animal or a symbol of your patron deity, to make it even more personal.

Finding a Mirror to Reflect Your Witchy Style

Some people like to enchant a Hexenspiegel for their home, protecting not only themselves but their family, property, and even home business from harm. For a home Hexenspiegel, a small mirror or mirrored item is just the thing. Look for a mirrored tree ornament; I found one that's a three-dimensional star, perfect for a Hexenspiegel. Watch for a mirrored decorative piece you can enchant and hang in a window or place in a prominent area of your home.

Mirrored Boxes

There are three kinds of mirrored boxes: boxes mirrored on the inside, boxes mirrored on the outside, and the infinity mirror box, which is a specific type of box with two mirrors placed strategically inside. When you think about where the mirrors are reflecting, you can get an idea of which box works for which purpose.

Let's explore the witch's mirrored box. Generally speaking, boxes mirrored on the inside hold energy in; boxes mirrored on the outside bounce energy away. A box mirrored on the inside can be used to destroy negativity or trap something; it's reflecting whatever is inside and bouncing its energy all over the inside of the box, thus keeping its energy there, like a loop. While boxes mirrored on the inside are sometimes used in revenge spells to bind and trap a person, I won't be describing how to do that here. There are uses for mirror boxes to make positive changes in your life; for example, a box mirrored on the inside can be employed to misdirect incoming negative energy into the box and trap it there.

Finding a box with mirrors on the inside to be used for magic may be a bit of a challenge, but such a thing isn't too hard to make. You don't have to cover the inside of the box entirely with a mirrored surface; you can paint the inside of the box black and then fit one mirror on each side, bottom and the lid, six total. If you're good at cutting glass, you can certainly make an entirely mirrored box. Some people cover the inside of a box with shards of broken mirrors or mirrored tiles. There are some boxes with fully mirrored interiors available online from voodoo and hoodoo shops. If you choose a premade one instead of making your own, as with all mirrors, first use a mirror purifier to make sure your box will be in line with the magical intention you want to set for it.

A box mirrored on the outside reflects incoming energies away from whatever is inside; therefore, it's good for hiding secrets, keeping something safe, or making something invisible or unnoticeable through a concealment spell. Boxes mirrored on the outside are perfect for creating a protective shield for a person or item and keep it safe from harm by placing an image or representation inside through sympathetic magic.

You can sometimes find boxes with mirrors on the outside in home decor stores, craft stores, even secondhand stores. These boxes can be completely covered with mirrors,

Finding a Mirror to Reflect Your Witchy Style

or decorated with a few mirrors and beads on all sides like those fancy, brightly colored lac mirrored boxes from India. Look for those in shops that carry imported gifts from all over the world. You can also decorate a premade box with mirrors, glue on simple small mirrored tiles, or create an elegant mosaic box using tile grout.

Another kind of mirrored box is an infinity mirror box. This kind of box has only two mirrors inside, both on opposite sides of the box, reflecting each other. In feng shui it's warned that hanging two mirrors directly across from each other and creating an infinity mirror effect can be unsettling in your home, as the energies bounce off each other and go into infinity. Take that concept and put it within the constraints of a mirror box, however, and you can magically benefit from this infinite reflection. The infinity mirror box can be used for multiplying anything; it's a great one for money magic. Properly enchanted boxes mirrored on the inside are great for creating a money-growing charm or multiplying anything you like. This is a box you're not likely to find anywhere and will probably have to make yourself, but as far as skills go, it's no harder than gluing two small mirrors to the inside of a box.

If you don't have a box you want to use to construct these mirror boxes already, you can usually find a little box at a secondhand, dollar, or craft store. Look for wooden or papier-mâché boxes; as an even more utilitarian option, cardboard shoeboxes will work. Two mirrors to attach on the inside can be found in the candle section of most dollar stores or big-box stores, which usually offer small mirrors for setting a candle on, and they often aren't very expensive. If all else fails, you can line the inside of a box with aluminum foil. Yeah, it's kinda down and dirty, but remember: modern glass mirrors are backed with aluminum. I've used aluminum foil for mirror magic in a pinch on several occasions, and it worked very well, so aluminum foil is witch tested and witch approved!

MIRROR LORE
For beauty, charge a round mirror
by the full moon and use that mirror
when you put on your makeup.

Compact Mirrors: Small but Mighty

Compact mirrors are a great go-to witch's mirror. They are really handy because of their size, so you can have one with you everywhere you go. These versatile little powerhouses can be used for all kinds of quick magic.

Finding a Mirror to Reflect Your Witchy Style

If the mirror can lay nice and flat without wobbling, you can place any small spell candle on the mirror. Flip the other side up behind the candle so that it reflects the candle from both the bottom and the side, increasing the power of any spell by reflecting and duplicating it! Reflect a magical gaze across the room; enchant your mirror for beauty or self-esteem; or fold up a dollar bill and place it, along with a mint leaf, inside the compact, turning it into a miniature infinity mirror for a quick prosperity spell. You can even use it for a quick psychic shield in a pinch. Pull it out of your purse to check your makeup, silently activate it to shield you and deflect harm, snap it shut, and then drop it back into your purse—it will still work from within your purse.

If you check out specialty New Age/metaphysical and online shops, you can find a huge variety of compact mirrors with magical symbols like moons, pentagrams, goddesses, and more to add a little extra mojo to your mirror. You can even find a simple compact in the health and beauty section of most big-box stores, then decorate it yourself or just leave it plain and incognito.

Witchy Wisdom on Real and Faux Mercury Glass

Mercury glass, also known as silvered glass, comes in the forms of items like candleholders, vases, or ornaments. It became very popular in the mid-1800s as the process of mirror making became perfected. Mercury glass items are great for working protection magic and can be enchanted to magically raise the vibrations of an area.

Mercury glass was hand blown with a double wall; a silvering formula was applied between the walls through a small hole in the bottom and then sealed or plugged. The formula did not actually contain mercury; it was called mercury glass due to its shiny mercury-like finish, although with the common name use, much like the Mercury dime, it does carry some minor Mercury influence in his aspect of the magician adding good luck, abundance, and success. Mercury glass also carries moon goddess energies, radiating positive energy for blessing and protection throughout your home.

Mercury glass pieces were originally created to duplicate the look of actual expensive silver so that everyone could have opulent-looking table settings for a fraction of the price of silver. They were sought after to bring joy and beautify the homes of the upper middle class, and many became family heirlooms. If you want to bring mercury glass items into your home to work mirror magic, you might be able to find pieces at antique stores or online, but you might pay a pretty penny for such a find as real mercury glass.

That being said, mercury glass is making a big comeback in the world of interior decor; you can find beautiful examples of faux mercury glass everywhere these days to fit almost every

Antique mirror & mercury glass items

budget. If you do an Internet search for mercury glass, more of the new faux versions come up than the original vintage ones. If you're out thrifting or at an auction and you're not sure if you've found the real thing or a modern faux reproduction, you can usually tell by how thick the glass is. The real antiques are double-walled glass, so they'll be thicker, with the silver coating the inside of the double walls. The new reproductions are usually, but not always, just single-walled thick glassware with coating right on the inside of the item, although a few modern manufacturers duplicate the double wall also.

If shopping for mercury glass online, look out for words like *antiqued*, meaning made to look old, versus *antique*, which should mean that it's actually old, at least if the seller is being honest. One of the hallmarks of mercury glass is the spots we see within the bright, shiny silver. The antique pieces usually have a wax or cork seal to protect the silver inside of the double wall. If these seals become compromised, tarnishing of the silver within can occur, causing the spots that we see. If you find a piece with a bad seal, you can replace the plug with a small cork or soft wax. That's a good reason to never submerge real mercury glass in water, just clean it gently with water and vinegar on a soft cloth. Another sign that it's probably a modern reproduction would be relatively evenly spaced spots; the real antiques don't usually spot evenly.

Finding a Mirror to Reflect Your Witchy Style

For magical purposes, does it matter if it's modern or antique? I've gotten amazing results from modern faux mercury glass, so I must report an adamant *nope*—it doesn't matter at all. The only reason it might be important to know the difference would be to assure that you get the most for your money when you're shopping.

If you want to try your hand at making your own faux mercury candleholders, ornaments, vases, etc., it's pretty easy to do, and my biggest warning to you is that it's highly addictive! I'll explain the process in chapter 6; you're going to totally love it! I used the method to create a mercury glass candleholder for house cleansing and an *oeil de sorcière*—then I was totally hooked on the process and wanted to turn all the glass in the world into cool-looking, sparkling mercury glass! You have been warned.

Oeil de Sorcière Mirrors

Speaking of the *oeil de sorcière* (roughly pronounced "oy de sorce-yere"), how gorgeous is this style of witch's mirror? There's nothing that shines the light of protection and blessings, as well as makes your space look witchy-cool, like an *oeil de sorcière*. These French-style convex, curved silver mirrors from the sixteenth century were all the rage amongst the wealthy in northern Europe. They're seen in many famous paintings and have also been called sorcerer's eye, witch's eye, and even god's eye mirrors due to their use as magical charms to ward against negativity and also offering blessings to the household as a watchful, benevolent eye. They were also status symbols during the early Renaissance period, so they can also be enchanted for prosperity magic.

I've seen some amazing antique *oeil de sorcière* mirrors for sale, and the prices for curved mirrors this old are not for the faint of heart. If you have the means, they can be located at auction houses and online auctions for anywhere from a few hundred to thousands of dollars.

Another version of the convex mirror is the Federal-style "bull's-eye" mirrors, pieces of Americana inspired by the European versions but usually with an eagle perched on top; often the frames are wood and decorated with gold leaf. I've seen many mid-century reproductions priced under a hundred dollars. You can also find elegant modern convex mirrors. As always, keep your eyes open at garage sales and secondhand stores; you never know what you might find!

It seems like it would be complex to make your own *oeil de sorcière* mirror, but it's actually easier than you might think to make one that looks like a real antique. It's really no harder than making a concave black mirror or faux mercury glass; in fact, the crafting of an *oeil de sorcière* combines both of the techniques. Watch for bubble-glass frames in secondhand stores; I lucked out and found one at a local secondhand store that was from the 1940s, with a filigree frame that was made in Italy,

Finding a Mirror to Reflect Your Witchy Style

for less than four bucks! Bubble glass in matching frames can also be found online. I found a great supplier called Victorian Frame Company with many sizes and price ranges, but there are lots of other suppliers out there too.

Indian Torans: Magical Moroccan Chic

Indian torans are a very special kind of decor meant to bring blessings. My daughter had one of these pretty, boldly colored fabric pieces covered with little embroidered elephants, birds, flowers, and bright mirror work hanging over her bedroom door when she was a teenager. I always admired it, and it gave a lovely feeling to her special space, creating a sanctuary. Look for them anywhere you might find those cool hippie tapestries, as shops with lots of tie-dye skirts and beaded curtains are likely to carry torans.

Another great place to look is import shops where they carry lots of home decor items from all over the world. If you can't find any locally or at Pagan festivals, try just typing the words "Indian torans" into an Internet search; I found lots at major online sellers as well as online craft stores. They come in many styles, colors, and price ranges, so if this is something you want for your home, you shouldn't have too much trouble finding just the right one.

You can also make these if you have the talent for sewing and embroidery. If you decide to make your own you can find mirrors to add to your project by searching for "shisha mirrors" or "shisha mirror trim."

An Indian toran, candle on a mirror, and mirrored box

Bagua and Feng Shui Mirrors

Bagua mirrors are the convex or concave mirrors in special frames used for feng shui placement strictly outside the home. You can sometimes find them in New Age/metaphysical shops, or Asian markets near you might carry them if you're lucky.

There are entire online stores dedicated to feng shui supplies, so you can always get a bagua mirror from an online source. If you want to use a bagua mirror, find a seller that's knowledgeable and communicative so you can doublecheck with them before you purchase; they can help you make sure that you get the right thing and use the right placement of these very specific kinds of magic mirrors. These mirrors are the most misused tool in feng shui, so please, if you really think you need one, check with a feng shui expert first to make sure you're using it correctly for your specific situation.

Mirrors for general feng shui purposes can be found in feng shui specialty stores and New Age/metaphysical stores, but you can also use the small hexagon or round mirrors found in craft stores or the ones used as candle bases.

As you can see, witch's mirrors can be found in many places, and many can be crafted yourself too. If you're buying a mirror, be sure to spiritually cleanse it with a purifier, smudge stick, or other technique of your choosing to clear away wayward vibes before enchanting and dedicating it as your own magical tool or charm. After that, you're good to go!

The Magic Between the Mirrors

I'm fascinated by chaos theory and how this idea dovetails nicely with modern Witches' experiences of magic. When Witches raise power to cast spells, they send their intent out "into the cosmos" to become reality, and no one knows where the energy goes, how far it travels, and what it changes or becomes before reverberating back and causing the desired effect. I believe that magical energy moves through different dimensions on its journey, and I have a spellcasting technique that works with this idea.

Place two mirrors facing each other, and it will appear that both mirrors reflect into infinity. Actually this is not the case because the photons bouncing back and forth between the mirrors that we see as images will eventually break down.

However, the illusion remains, and so if you stand between the mirrors and look at your reflection multiplied, it will give you the sensation that you are looking at parallel universes through a portal. This creates a perfect setting for casting spells on yourself: you project the energy through one mirror and turn around to receive it from the other mirror. Visualize that this energy has traversed layers of time and space, morphing into magic as it returns and manifests your goal.

You can also use the same two-mirror setup to charge an object. I recommend a clear quartz since it can be programmed for any purpose and it has the proven ability to receive and transmit energy, which is why quartz is used in radios, clocks, computer chips, and other electronics. Apply the process described above and channel the returning energy into the quartz, focusing on your intent. This will create a potent magical tool for healing, banishing, clairvoyance, astral projection, or whatever function you attune it to. Again, this works best if you are going to use the empowered crystal on yourself.

People are always surprised when I tell them that science factors heavily into my Witchcraft beliefs, although I'm far from being a Technopagan. My personal scrying mirror, for example, is pretty old-school. It's a two- by three-inch polished flat oval hematite palm stone, closer to the ancient ritual obsidian mirrors used in Mesoamerica than to an actual looking glass. Scrying with modern-day mirrors has never really worked for me, so I prefer to use them more for magic than for divination.

Autumn Damiana
Writer, artist, crafter, and amateur photographer • visit her blog, Sacred Survival in a Mundane World, at http://autumndamiana.blogspot.com

Finding a Mirror to Reflect Your Witchy Style

chapter
6

Crafting and Enchanting
a Witch's Mirror

By now you've probably figured out what kind of witch's mirror (or mirrors) you want. We all know witches tend to be crafty people, so if you're one of those witches who likes to make your own magical tools, I think you'll really enjoy making your own witch's mirror. I've made some myself, and it's very rewarding. You don't have to pick just one; mirrors are a wonderful kind of magic that you can use in many areas of your life and magical practice. Let your imagination run wild, grab your paint, glass, and glue gun, and make some magic all your own. Even if you're lucky enough to find a witch's mirror to purchase, you're going to need to enchant it for your purpose; all the methods for enchanting a handcrafted mirror can be used to enchant a store-purchased mirror as well. Read on as we get our witchy craft on!

Make Your Own Black Scrying Mirror

Black mirrors are not as difficult to make as you might think. With a little care and patience, you can craft a really nice black witch's mirror. Here are the basics.

First, you'll need a piece of clear glass. If you want a classic concave black mirror, you can use a convex clock glass or convex glass made for antique frames, also known as bubble glass or domed glass. I've had great luck with Victorian Frame Company, but there are lots of good places to find curved glass, such as a clock repair supply shop. Remember, what you're looking for is called convex glass because that's how they sell it, but we will be flipping it around and using the other side, using the concave side for viewing. Once you've got your glass, be sure to clean it well using the new mirror purifier from chapter 7 on both sides of the glass.

You'll also need some black paint. Lots of people suggest using black spray paint, and that does work fine; I've tried it. If you want to just pick up a can of black enamel spray paint, be sure to apply it in several thin coats on the convex (back) side of the mirror.

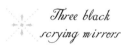

Three black scrying mirrors

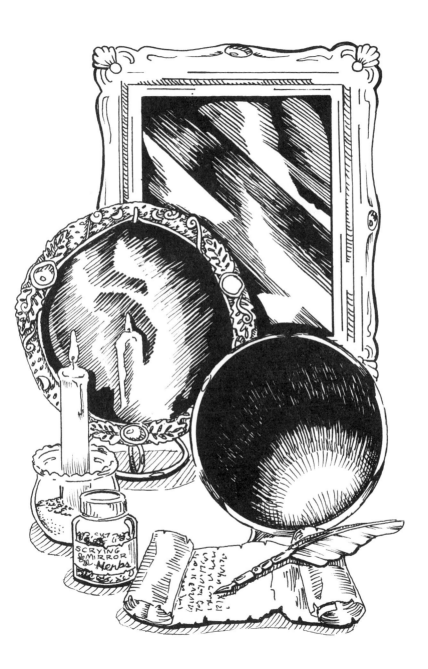

SCRYING
MIRROR
Herbs

A new trick I discovered is using acrylic enamel paint that's suitable for glass instead of spray paint. There are lots of affordable brands; they're generally sold in little two-ounce bottles; the one I use is made by Folk Art. It's easy to clean up, there are no poisonous fumes or overspray, plus working with water-based washes or fluid condensers isn't a problem if you choose a water-based paint instead of an oil-based paint. Because you're brushing it on the back of the glass, you'll be using several coats applied with a soft, large brush that is at least an inch wide to minimize brush strokes. Even if you do see slight brushstrokes on the back, they won't be seen at all on the glass side of the mirror where you'll be doing your scrying. As a magical bonus, on your last coat of paint you could leave brushstrokes on purpose in the shapes of magical symbols; they will impart their energies to the mirror but remain invisible from the front.

Whether you choose black spray paint or water-based glass paint, you'll need to choose your magic mirror wash or condenser, decide your preference, and mix up your choice of enchantment for your mirror and have it ready. Formulas are in chapter 7. If you're using the solid scrying mirror condenser from chapter 7, instructions for including the solid condenser are included with the formula.

As far as timing, I like to make my scrying mirrors during a significant moon phase, either the dark moon or the full moon. I usually plan for the two days surrounding the moon phase I'm working in, as I often need time to let paint dry, make a frame, etc., and I don't want to feel rushed on decorative details. Many people like to follow the old tradition of not allowing sunlight to fall upon a black mirror, so I make mine at night just to be on the safe side, but do use a well-lit area when you apply the black paint.

Set up your supplies in a clean area and put down newspaper on your work surface to protect it from black paint. If you're using a mirror wash, apply it to the surface before you paint the first layer on the convex side of the glass, rubbing in a counterclockwise direction and wiping it completely dry. If you're using the simple fluid condenser instead of mirror wash, you'll need a jar with a little condenser in the bottom. Use your paint brush to apply a very thin layer of condenser onto the back of your mirror glass. A little bit of condenser goes a long way—this is very powerful stuff. Dry your brush well on a paper towel, then apply your first layer of paint while your condenser is still damp. If using spray paint, be sure to allow the condenser to dry completely before painting; remember, oil and water don't mix. Spray paints are oil based.

It's best to apply the paint in several thin layers, allowing it to dry in between layers; usually three layers is good. Rinse and dry your paintbrush in between layers. If in doubt, after three layers hold it up to a light. If you can see light through

Crafting and Enchanting a Witch's Mirror

it, apply one more coat. Allow the paint to dry completely; this may not be completely dry until the next night. Check the paint label for details on drying times and curing if necessary, and follow them exactly before proceeding to the next step.

If you're using spray paint, you may wish to apply a thin layer of varnish for extra protection from getting scratched. If you use acrylic enamel, try the oven-curing method; according to the directions on the paint, this protects it wonderfully. Some people might prefer to adhere a round piece of felt on the back for extra protection. A very tacky craft glue such as Aleen's works great for gluing felt to glass. Felt is a tricky fabric to glue, so a thick, tacky craft glue works great. Cut the felt slightly smaller than the size of the mirror. Apply the glue with a brush evenly over the already painted surface of your black mirror. You may want to include a sprinkling of herbs or a tad more condenser to the glue.

Instead of felt, here's my favorite way to protect the back of a scrying mirror and make an elegant and personal frame. I have had great success by crafting a sculpted custom frame made of oven-bake polymer clay such as Fimo or Sculpy. You can actually work some of the dry powdered herbs you used in the wash or condenser into the clay itself. Do not try to mix mirror wash or fluid condenser into polymer clay—it will go horribly wrong—but a pinch of dried herbs or solid condenser (the powdered one) is fine. Then use a rolling pin to roll the clay to about a quarter-inch thickness and slightly larger than the scrying mirror on a sheet of wax paper so it doesn't stick to your workspace. Press it over the painted surface of the mirror and carefully work it around to the front edge, forming about a half-inch-thick frame. Now you can decorate the front part of the frame by pressing patterns into the clay, adding small tumbled stones such as moonstones, obsidian, or quartz, or even seashells. Bake the entire mirror according to the instructions on the polymer clay package.

Once it's completely cooled, you can brush it with acrylic paint a small section at a time and rub it off while the paint is still wet, leaving paint in all the crevices and creating an antiqued look. If you get any paint on the front of the mirror (which you will, trust me), just add a little water to the paint with a clean brush and wipe it off with a paper towel or a cotton swab to get in close to the edges. Once you're finished, coat the clay with some clear water-based varnish. I like a satin finish, but this is, of course, your choice.

You can pick up an inexpensive wooden easel to place it in while scrying. You might be inspired to decorate it with a wood burner. A wire easel can be equally nice and is easily decorated by wrapping it with silver wire and magical beads and charms of your choice.

If you don't have the resources to make a convex mirror or you just prefer a flat one, you can use the steps above and

Crafting and Enchanting a Witch's Mirror

simply substitute a piece of flat glass. Find a beautiful picture frame that includes a piece of glass. Use the mirror wash or condenser of your choice and apply at least three coats of glass paint to one side of the glass in the same way that's described in the instructions for the concave mirror. Once it's completely dry, insert the glass back into its frame, painted side to the back. It's a really easy and beautiful way to create an amazing witch's tool that you'll use and treasure for years.

If you mail-ordered curved glass and the packaging it came in was nice, that packaging might be great for storing your finished mirror. You could cover the box with elegant paper and wrap your mirror in silk, linen, or some nice fabric before placing it in the protective box with the padding. You can also design your own packaging, being careful to protect it from direct sunlight.

Do not allow others to handle or use your scrying mirror; this will keep its energies aligned closely with your own. The best time to scry is during a full or a dark moon. You can use mirror wash to clean the front of the mirror or any time you feel the need to boost the magic power of your scrying mirror.

Open the Black Mirror Portal— What Do You See?

Before using your mirror for the first time, whether you crafted it yourself or purchased it, make sure it's clean. Try working with it on the night of a full or dark moon, which tends to bring powerful visions. Place the mirror on the stand facing you. Place the open palm of your receptive hand before the mirror and move your hand in a clockwise circle. Put the open palm of your other hand behind the mirror and "mirror" the action of your receptive hand so that you have one hand in front and one hand behind the mirror, both palms facing each other and moving in a clockwise pattern. As you do this, visualize the mirror becoming a portal for visions to be drawn to you. Thus, your mirror is aligned with your energies and spiritually magnetized for the purpose of scrying. When you are finished using your mirror, repeat the hand motions above in reverse to close the portal and give thanks for your visions.

After preparing the mirror as described above, place your scrying mirror on a clean cloth on a table or altar at eye level in a dark room or under the stars. You may burn incense aligned with lunar energies or specially formulated for scrying; a few recommendations are sandalwood, frankincense, jasmine, or nag champa. Place two candles, one on either side of the mirror, arranging them so that they do not reflect in the surface of the mirror. The surface of the mirror should be completely black in order to see visions when scrying. Have a sheet of paper or a journal and a pen handy to record any of your impressions in order to contemplate them later. Much like a dream, details of visions can be forgotten quickly if they are not recorded immediately.

Crafting and Enchanting a Witch's Mirror

Cast a circle of protection around your work space, visualizing a protective circle of blue flames or a clear bubble surrounding you. (If you are not familiar with casting a circle, please refer to a book on basic magic before proceeding.) You may invite your spirit guides to join you, specifically asking only spirits in line with your own intentions to enter your circle. Ground and center yourself, and relax into a meditative state. Gaze into the glass surface, relaxing your eyes and looking deeply into and through the surface. Use the mirror as a focal point—a portal to a place where all that is or will be known can be seen by you. Most people "see" without their physical eyes when scrying; you may only receive impressions, shadows, and visions in the mist, and may need much practice as well as reflection to interpret these visions. You may wish to consult a dream dictionary to look into symbolism that you may see while scrying. I have included a small reference guide at the back of this book to get you started; see appendix 2. Relax, don't force it, and remember: the more often you practice, the easier visions will come to you.

When you are finished, thank your spirit guides and respectfully ask them to return to their realms, harming none along the way. Place your right palm in front of the mirror and your left hand behind it, moving them as you did before but this time counterclockwise three times, declaring the portal closed. Visualize the protective circle dissipating. Put out the candles and carefully return the mirror to its protective packaging of your choice. Store your mirror out of reach of others until your next use.

Crafting Hexenspiegel Jewelry and Suncatchers

A mirrored necklace, bracelet, or a mirrored ornament can be made into a Hexenspiegel with a simple bit of magic that I'll share with you here. The Hexenspiegel can be worn, carried in your purse or wallet, or displayed in your home to ward off curses, hexes, or psychic attacks. The beautiful part of the Hexenspiegel is that the thing just works all the time, meaning that if someone decides to pull some shady stuff on you,

Crafting and Enchanting a Witch's Mirror

Hexenspiegel jewelry

the minute they tap into your energy they're going to know right away that you're protected and more than likely decide to stop their shenanigans before they begin. And if a magical bully decides to cause you harm and then chooses not to recoil from the attack once they feel the protection in place, that's their free will to do so; the Hexenspiegel will just do its thing.

To make a simple Hexenspiegel necklace, you'll need a small square or round glass tile from your local craft store. You can get these in little bags that often can be found near the stained glass or mosaic supplies. You'll also need a small bit of polymer oven bake clay; I use Sculpy, but Fimo or another brand will work just fine. You'll need a short piece of wire to make a loop (or bail) to hang it from. You can also work a pinch of a protection herb of your choice right into the clay. A few suggestions include powdered vervain, dill, rosemary, marjoram, holly leaves or berries, rowan, mullein, or nettle; use only dried herbs and don't try to add oils or mirror wash to the clay. For this purpose a very small pinch of herbs goes a long way, so don't use too much. You can also draw a protection symbol such as a pentagram or triquetra onto the back of the mirror using a fine-pointed permanent marker before adding the clay.

Take a piece of clay and work a pinch of your protection herbs into it by kneading it with your fingers. Pinch off a bit of

Crafting and Enchanting a Witch's Mirror

clay that's big enough to cover one side of the tile and roll the clay out flat to about a quarter of an inch thick. Lay the tile on top of the clay and trim the clay so that it's the same size as the tile. Form the wire into a loop and slide it in between the clay and the back of the mirror; this is how you will hang it from a necklace. Now roll out a long coil of clay about as thick as a spaghetti noodle. Starting at the top, where the wire is, roll the coil around the outside edge of the mirror tile. When you reach the wire loop again, wrap the coil around the tile one more time, but this time it should be around the front side of the mirror, creating a tiny frame. To end the coil back up at the top of the pendant, break off the clay and leave a pretty little spiral at the end.

If you wish, you can use clay stamps or a piece of jewelry to stamp designs or texture into the clay. Bake your Hexenspiegel pendant according to the directions for your clay. Once it's cool you may paint it or leave it natural. If you decide to paint your pieces and you get paint on the mirror while you work, which is pretty much unavoidable, just drop a little water on the mirror while the paint is still wet and clean it off with a couple clean cotton swabs. Also, I like to carefully apply a coat of water-based varnish to my polymer projects to give the paint some extra protection. Now decide if you want to hang it from a simple chain or cord, or create a beaded necklace with the Hexenspiegel as the centerpiece. Get as creative as you want—you could even make two small ones into earrings!

Another easy-to-make Hexenspiegel is a suncatcher Hexenspiegel. This is a Hexenspiegel you can hang in your window to deflect negativity and ward your whole home. To make this especially enchanted ornamental protection mirror, you'll need six or eight craft tile mirrors, ¾-inch size or so, and some strong craft glue such as E6000 adhesive or a two-part epoxy. Really, any adhesive that's pretty strong and preferably waterproof and appropriate for glass will work. You'll also need 40-pound fishing line and a metal or crystal charm of about 1 inch to hang at the bottom. You'll also need a handful of beads; good choices would include (but are not limited to) blue or green glass evil eye beads, jasper, quartz, black tourmaline, turquoise, or amethyst.

Cut about a foot and a half or so of fishing line and tie your charm to one end using a fishing knot; you can find some examples of these on the Internet. Here's a beading trick: open a large hardbound book that lays flat on its own and use the fold in the middle (the gutter) where the pages meet to lay your beads out in the order you want to bead them; you can lay your mirror tiles out in the arrangement too. I make them about 9–12 inches long, including beads and mirrors, but we have a foot and a half of fishing line, right? Yep, that's so you have plenty of extra for easily knotting both ends.

Begin stringing beads in order from the bottom where the charm is to the top, and attach a clothespin or office clip

Crafting and Enchanting a Witch's Mirror

about four inches from the other end to keep the beads from accidentally sliding off. Laying the beaded line flat on a table, choose several areas to add your mirrors, spacing the beads out just enough to accommodate them. Starting at the bottom, lay one mirror, shiny side down, under the empty space in the fishing line between the beads, then add a dot of adhesive in the center of the mirror and make sure the fishing line is stuck in the center of the adhesive. Sprinkle the adhesive with your Hexenspiegel protective herbs. Now lay another mirror on top of it so that the two tiles are back to back, with the fishing line and magic herbs sandwiched in between. Proceed in the same way, spacing mirrors all along the line between sections of beads. When you're done, walk away and leave it alone. I know it's pretty but just leave it there and forget about it for at least two hours. Is this the voice of experience? Yes, it is; trust me, and leave it undisturbed while the mirrors dry. Once you're sure they are completely dry (check the manufacturer's directions on your adhesive), wrap the other end around a cork and use that fishing knot again. Slide out the cork and you've got a nice loop for hanging.

Now you'll want to enchant your Hexenspiegel to become a magical shield for your home. Here's a charm that you can use to turn any mirror, mirrored jewelry, or mirrored item like an ornament into a working Hexenspiegel. It's a simple enchantment, and once you've used it you don't have to do anything else; your Hexenspiegel will continue to do its job. It's a vigilant little mirror with a powerful intention—to warn your enemies not to attack—and if they do, it packs up that energy and hands it right back where it came from, leaving you in a constant state of magical protection.

Apply Hexenspiegel mirror wash (the recipe is in chapter 7) on your new piece and wipe it clean with a paper towel or cotton cloth. Light a white candle and set your new Hexenspiegel next to it. Say:

> *Hexenspiegel, my witch's charm*
> *Become my shield from any harm*
> *Warn my attackers to retreat*
> *Should they persist, I do entreat*
> *Reflect their evil away from me*
> *To which I add no energy*
> *And what they send returned shall be*
> *As by my will so shall it be*

Now your Hexenspiegel is ready to go. Wear your jewelry anytime or keep it by your bed when you're not wearing it. Hang your suncatcher in a window using a suction cup or a hook above the window. Under normal circumstances you shouldn't need to do a thing—it will just continue to work; however, if you feel the need you can always repeat the enchanting charm, adding a spritz of Hexenspiegel mirror wash to boost its effectiveness.

Crafting and Enchanting a Witch's Mirror

Make Mirrored Boxes: Magic Inside and Out

A mirrored box can be as aesthetically pleasing or as utilitarian as you want it to be. If you plan to leave it out on a shelf, you'll probably want to make it look nice. If you're going to keep it in a drawer or cabinet, you could literally just glue some mirrors to the outside of a box and it will be equally magical, even if it's not very pretty.

Box Mirrored on the Outside

A box with mirrors on the outside is a great tool for spellwork to keep something hidden from view or notice. It can also shield objects from soaking up negative energy from outside sources. This works great for things like magical jewelry, keys to your magical cabinet, or your oils for spellwork.

You can also use representations of things you want to keep safe, such as a photo of something you want to hide or shield. If you're worried about others messing with your phone, use a photo of your phone—your actual phone—not just a picture of a model phone. When you get a new credit or debit card and peel the sticker off to activate it, stick the sticker onto a piece of paper and put it in the box to protect your account from being compromised. Of course, you still need to use common sense to protect your stuff in the mundane world, but the mirrored box will certainly help. Basically, if it's yours and you want others to leave it alone, put it or a photo of it into a box with mirrors on the outside.

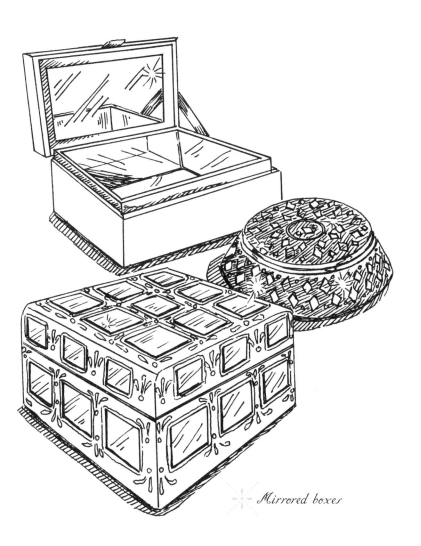

Mirrored boxes

Now, keep in mind that it won't render something literally invisible, but this kind of mirrored box can make an object unnoticeable. If you know it's there you'll see it, but otherwise it will just escape someone's notice, like a science fiction perception filter. Such a concealment spell can be very useful in many situations.

To make a simple box that's mirrored on the outside, you'll need a wooden or papier-mâché box from your local craft shop and enough small mirrored tiles to decorate it. You'll also need a bottle of regular acrylic craft paint and a tube of dimensional fabric paint in the same color. Using the flat and dimensional paint in the same color is much more forgiving when it's time to decorate with the dimensional paint; little errors look artistic instead of messy. For the dimensional paint I found a bottle of Tulip fabric paint that worked well for me, but any brand is fine as long as it's in a bottle that looks like a glue bottle with a nice pointy tip; I would avoid the kind that puffs up. Choose whatever color you like; I love the look of metallics—gold or silver look really cool—or black, or you might like to match it to your decor or choose a color that speaks to you. Matching your decor is actually a great idea—after all, this kind of mirrored spell box is all about camouflage.

Paint the outside of the box with the acrylic paint and let it dry. You might need two coats, and be sure you don't paint the box shut. Be careful to paint around hinges or any other hardware if your box has them; if you paint over those, they won't work. On the top of the box, lay out your mirror tiles in a nice pattern, making sure you leave at least a half inch between them. Lightly trace around the outside of each tile with a pencil for placement reference. One by one, affix the mirrors to the box using some premium tacky craft glue; my go-to is Aleene's but there are others out there too (watch for the term "tacky," that's what you want). You can also use industrial adhesive or hot glue if you prefer. Once all the tiles are attached to the lid, let them dry so they don't move around for the next step.

Now trace around each tile with a bead of the dimensional fabric paint right along the edge of each mirror. This covers the sharp edges of the mirrors, and each tile looks like it's set on the box with the paint, like a jewel. If there's a lot of space between some of the mirrors, you can decorate it with patterns of swirls, leaves, or mehndi designs (used in henna tattoos); you could even attach a few pretty glass beads, protective stones, or evil eye beads—get creative and add your own personal style. The dimensional paint will have a whitish cast to the color but will become a more vivid color when it's dry.

Do one side of the box at a time, allowing the dimensional paint to dry for at least four hours before you move to the next side, being careful not to glue the lid closed with the

Crafting and Enchanting a Witch's Mirror

paint. When you're finished with the outside, you can put symbols inside the box for magical protection, such as an equal-armed cross, pentagram, or triquetra, or include symbols for invisibility, such as Hulinhjálmur or Solomon's Sixth Seal of the Sun. Be sure to check out the backing images and magical seals at the end of chapter 8.

Once your box is completely dry—give that dimensional paint seventy-two hours to be sure—then you can lightly spray some protection mirror wash onto a soft cloth, making it just slightly damp, and wipe it all over the outside of the box. Now your witch's mirror box is ready to use.

Box Mirrored on the Inside

Boxes mirrored on the inside are great for destroying negativity or trapping something. If you're making a mirrored box for these purposes, you'll need all six sides of the inside of the box to be mirrored. While the entire surface of the inside of the box doesn't have to be mirrored, there should be at least one mirror on every side, and the rest of the inside should be painted black or silver.

Another type of box mirrored on the inside is meant for the purpose of multiplying something. If you're making a box for multiplying something—for instance, money—it should only have two mirrors on the inside, across from each other, each reflecting the other so that they create an infinity mirror.

Mirrors can be attached to the inside of a box using a good strong adhesive; I like to use a tube of industrial-strength adhesive, something flexible, paintable, and waterproof. Apply masking tape to hold the mirror in place while the glue dries. Decorate the outside of the box any way you wish. You might want to decorate it according to the purpose of the box. If you're making it to trap negativity inside, you might like to paint it black, glue on metal keys, and paint vertical lines suggesting bars or use other symbols such as equal-armed crosses or pentagrams as seals. For an infinity mirror box, you could use colors of what you plan to multiply; for money, use shades of green, silver, and gold or fancy scrapbook paper featuring coins from around the world. If you want to multiply personal power, paint it your favorite color, decoupage your spirit animal, and attach your birthstone and other emblems that represent you.

Create Your Own Faux Mercury Glass and Oeil de Sorcière

You are seriously going to love the process of making faux mercury glass. The method is as magical as the results you get creating beautiful sparkling candleholders, vases, etc., to magically fill your home with good vibes and blessings! You can also use the same technique to make a really cool antique-looking *oeil de sorcière*.

Oeil de sorcière mirrors &
faux mercury glass jar candles

If you want to use magical timing, you can make your mercury glass on a Wednesday to channel Mercury's energy, including good luck, fertility (literal or figurative), abundance, and success. You can also make it on Monday for associations with silver and the moon, since silver was actually an ingredient in most antique mercury glass. Most items actually didn't contain mercury at all and were simply called mercury glass as a holdover from when mercury was actually used in mirror making and the mercury-like look of the pieces. Creating mercury glass on a Monday would add energies of the moon goddess, protection, healing, psychic powers, and love. Either way you choose, a faux mercury glass item made magically will be a blessing to your home, radiating positive energy.

Let's start with a mercury glass candleholder. The first one I made was a jelly jar, and it turned out looking really cool and rustic. I made it especially for a family I was doing a house blessing and cleansing for as an extra enchantment they could use anytime they needed to raise the vibes of the home once we kicked out the astral nasties. They use it all the time and have not had any of the entities we sent packing return, and the energy of the home has remained very uplifting. You can use a jar too, if you like, or find a beautiful clear vase, drinking glass, or glass hurricane lamp shade. If you have one special piece, I suggest you practice on another piece first, like a simple jar, to get the knack of it.

Clean your glass jar with mirror purifier, then dry it. You'll need a can of mirror finish spray paint, mercury glass wash (see chapter 7) in a spray bottle, masking tape, newspaper, paper towels, and a clean ventilated area with a table top protected with newspaper where you can work. You might be tempted to grab a can of silver chrome paint, but it will not have the shine of the spray paint designed to create a mirror-like finish on glass; I used one called Looking Glass by Krylon that worked really well. At the time there were no other brands but that one, but I just saw another one pop up this month and more are likely to follow. Read the cans carefully and be sure it says specifically that it's mirror paint so you get the right stuff.

Tape a piece of newspaper around the outside of your jar, using the masking tape right up to the lip of the jar, protecting the outside of the jar completely from any overspray. Before you begin, shake the spray paint for about two minutes. I can't stress this enough: if you want it to be as bright as possible, you really need to shake the heck out of that can! The metallic substance settles quickly, so you'll want to shake it vigorously between sprays as well.

Spritz the inside of your jar with mercury glass wash—just a bit; less is more. Now shake the can well and give the inside of the jar a light coating of mirror finish spray paint. Allow it to dry about four to five minutes, then blot it with a crumpled-up paper towel. This will remove the paint from the spots where the water droplets are, leaving the signature spots that we see on antique mercury glass. If you like a more aged look, you can apply a bit more pressure and give the paper towel little twists to remove a bit more paint. Now repeat the steps of spritzing with mercury glass wash, spraying the mirror paint, and blotting three or four more times until it looks exactly how you want. If you accidentally remove too much silver, you can just respray it a bit. If you didn't leave as many spots as you wanted, spray with water one last time and use a crumpled paper towel in small twisting patterns to remove more paint.

Once you're happy with it, allow it to dry for at least twenty-four hours. When you burn a candle inside your new mercury glass, you boost its powers, allowing light to shine through the silver finish as it emanates good vibes and reflects them at the same time, becoming a beacon of positive energy. Now you just have to resist the urge to turn everything in your house into faux mercury glass! Keep your mercury glass wash and use it whenever you clean your faux mercury glass or anytime you feel it needs a magical boost.

To make an *oeil de sorcière*, you will use the same technique described above; the only differences are the glass you start with and you will use the witch's eye mirror wash (see chapter 7) instead of the mercury glass wash. If you're a lucky

Crafting and Enchanting a Witch's Mirror

shopper, you might find a good bubble glass frame at a secondhand store or online; if you can't find an inexpensive used one, Victorian Frame Company has a nice variety of sizes and frames as well, or just do an Internet search for "vintage bubble glass frame" and you'll find lots of resources.

Follow the same steps in the instructions for making the mercury glass jar, spraying the concave (bowl side) of the glass. When it's dry and you're ready to mount it in the frame, you may wish to boost the *oeil de sorcière*'s properties by adding a backing image of a magical symbol in the frame behind the glass (there are a few at the end of chapter 8). You can also add a sprinkling of protective and blessing herbs like angelica, sage, rowan, or rue inside the actual frame.

Place the *oeil de sorcière* in a prominent location in your home and it will do its job bringing down blessings from Spirit, watching over your household, and deflecting any harmful energy from you and your home to become neutral and harmless energy free from ill intent.

Use the witch's eye mirror wash anytime you clean it or feel the need to boost its enchantment. The mirror also acts as a warning bell in your psychic mind and will let you know through your own intuition if it needs a boost to keep doing its job well. The *oeil de sorcière* is a powerful witch's tool indeed!

Psychomanteum:
A Spirit Communication Mirror

Communication with spirits through mirrors is an age-old practice. During the Victorian era they called a darkened chamber with a spirit communication mirror a "psychomanteum." I've come up with a way to enchant a mirror for use in a similar technique, thus adding power and intention to the mirror itself.

Enchanting a mirror just for this purpose can be handy if it's something you plan to do often. A black mirror can be used to communicate across the veil, but you can also use a silver mirror. Here, I will describe how to enchant an everyday silver mirror for spirit communication. If you only plan to use a mirror for this purpose occasionally, you can temporarily use an altar mirror for this purpose and then close the portal by removing those elements after you're done.

If you want to add power through magical timing, work at the dark of the moon or on a Wednesday. Samhain or Beltane would be good sabbats to work on when making a spirit communication mirror, since the veil between the worlds is thinnest during these times.

You'll need a mirror at least twelve by twelve inches, although it doesn't have to be a square mirror and it should be in a removable frame. Take the mirror out of the frame and cleanse both front and back with mirror purifier wash. Now use the spirit communication wash in chapter 7 on the back of the mirror only. Make a copy of the spirit gate seal found at the end of chapter 8 or trace it using black ink onto white paper. Using masking tape to cover all the edges, tape the backing seal facedown in the center of the mirror's back. Put the open palm of your right hand over the back of the mirror and the top of the backing sigil about an inch away from the glass, and move your hand in a counterclockwise motion. As you do this, visualize the mirror opening from the back across the veil. It remains sealed in the front until you activate it. Now cover the entire back of the mirror with a piece of black paper. You can use black poster board or construction paper cut to the size and shape of the mirror. Now place the mirror back into the frame with the original board on the back covering the black paper and backing seal.

This mirror should be stored wrapped in black cloth when not in use. It will remain inactive until you use the spirit communication wash on the front of the mirror and activate it by placing your left palm about an inch over the surface and moving it in a clockwise motion over the mirror while evoking the mirror to open. You can use this mirror for communication with loved ones who have crossed over, familiar spirits, spirit guides, or even your patron deity.

Now you have a spirit communication mirror. This is the mirror used in the psychomanteum spirit contact spell in chapter 8. If you only want to temporarily use a mirror for spirit communication (this is probably how most people would do it), after you're done with your psychomanteum, close the front of the mirror with mirror purifier, take the backing off the frame, remove the spirit gate seal, and burn it, scattering the ashes in the wind. Use mirror purifier again all over the entire mirror.

Mirror of the Moon

A mirror charged with the energy of the full moon can be used specifically for moon magic. A moon mirror doubles the power of the rest of your spell elements, adding extra lunar energy to spells for love, healing, increasing magical power, intuition, and more. This moon mirror is usually placed flat on the altar while you're celebrating a full moon esbat or performing spells in which lunar energy is appropriate.

A moon mirror should be round and be between two to four inches in diameter. Try mirrors in the candle section of your favorite home decor or big box store; the round mirrors they have for candle bases are perfect. You can also find good-sized mirrors with finished edges in many craft stores. You'll also need a silver-colored paint pen and the lunar mirror wash in chapter 7. Use the silver paint pen to draw the mirror of the moon seal in chapter 8 on the back of the mirror. Take your mirror outside during a full moon. Use the lunar mirror wash on the front of the mirror and wipe it clean in a clockwise circle. Position the mirror on the ground so that you can see the reflection of the moon in the mirror. Surround the mirror with silver; the easiest way to do this is by using one or more silver chains and link them together to form a circle.

Stand over the mirror so that the moon is reflected in the mirror's surface. Now make a triangle of manifestation gesture. To make this gesture hold your fingers together and thumb apart like you're wearing mittens. Touch the tips of your index fingers and thumbs so that the space between your two hands forms a triangle. Now hold the triangle between the moon in the sky and the mirror reflecting it, allowing the moonlight to pass through the triangle and into the mirror. Focusing on the reflection of the moon through the triangle, repeat the following charm thirteen times, for the full moon occurs thirteen times in the year:

Speculo Lunae
Mirror of the night
Fill this looking glass
With your magical light

As you charge the mirror, feel the loving power of the moon surrounding you, flowing through your hands, and filling the mirror with that power as if it were a cup overflowing with white moonlight energy. You may leave the mirror to bask in the moonlight for as long as you like, but take care to bring it inside before the sun rises. Keep the mirror out of the sunlight. Protect it by wrapping it in a dark-colored scarf or putting it into a drawstring bag. The next time you're doing some big moon magic, bring out your moon mirror and let its power shine. Set candles on it on your full moon altar, place a petition on it and surround it with herbs for healing spells, and use it as a spell element anytime you want to add lunar energy to rituals or spellwork. Recharge it using the same method anytime you want, especially during a supermoon or blue moon.

Crafting and Enchanting a Witch's Mirror

Mirror of the Sun

A mirror charged with the power of the sun can be a great boost to spellwork for increasing prosperity, growing personal power, and boosting metabolism, joy, growth, and renewal. Mirrors also have been used at faraway distances to reflect the sunlight toward another person in order to send messages, so they're great for communication magic.

I have to start the instructions for making this special magic mirror with a warning, so bear with me here: never, ever, *ever* look directly at the sun's reflection, in a mirror or otherwise. You're not going to use the same method here as you did for the moon mirror. This one's a little different because you can wreck your eyes if you try to gaze at the sun. (You probably already knew that, but just in case you get excited about charging your sun mirror, it needed to be said.)

A sun mirror should also be round, like the moon mirror; two to four inches in diameter is a good size. The mirrors in the candle section of your favorite home decor or big box store work great—they have nice mirrors with beveled edges for candle bases. There are mirrors of the right size with finished edges in many craft stores. You'll also need a gold-colored paint pen and the solar mirror wash in chapter 7. Use the gold paint pen to draw the mirror of the sun seal (from chapter 8) on the back of the mirror. Charging your sun mirror at the time of the sun's zenith, at noon, will fill it with solar power. For more magical timing, try a Sunday. Making this mirror on the spring equinox (when the sun's power is beginning to grow) or the summer solstice at noon (the sun's most powerful position all year) would both be excellent. Use the solar mirror wash on the front of the mirror and wipe it clean in a clockwise circle.

Bring the mirror outside at noon on your chosen day and place it someplace where it's in direct sunlight. Surround the mirror with gold—try using one or more gold chains (gold plated is fine) and linking them together to form a circle around the mirror. Now make a triangle of manifestation gesture. The description of this gesture is in the moon mirror directions, but for this mirror you will be using it in a different way. Making sure that you are positioned where you can't see the sun's reflection in the mirror, hold the triangle of manifestation over the mirror so that the shadow your hands make is over the mirror and the triangle of sunlight is in the center of the mirror. Even though you aren't looking directly at the sun's reflection—which could damage your eyes; just don't do it—from the mirror's point of view the sun is right in the middle of your triangle, and that's all that matters.

Repeat the following charm eight times to represent the yearly stations of the sun in the solstices, equinoxes, and cross quarters:

Crafting and Enchanting a Witch's Mirror

Speculum Solis
Star of the day
Empower this glass
With each mighty ray

You don't need to leave it outside after your short ritual; the sun's rays absorb very quickly in a mirror. Store it wrapped in a gold-colored scarf or golden drawstring bag. The next time you're doing some magic for money, legal matters, communication, health, or any solar-related magic, set your sun mirror on the altar along with your herbs, stones, and candles and let it double everything with its sunny energy. Feel free to recharge it anytime you feel the need, and don't forget to set it outside next summer solstice!

Bad Vibe Trap

This is a special mirror used for trapping negative energy that's already built up within your environment. A Hexenspiegel or *oeil de sorcière* is great for deflecting incoming baneful energy, but what do you do if creepy, nasty vibes are already there? This no-nonsense mirror combines a reflective silvered mirror with a black back and becomes a negativity vacuum, like a black hole: bad energy goes in but can't come out. You need this one, right? It's more about function than fancy, but it's easy to make and a powerful way to clean house, spiritually speaking.

First you'll need black quick-dry nail polish, black electrical tape, and a concave silvered mirror. Any round mirror that magnifies will work, so check out the health and beauty section while you're shopping and watch for shaving mirrors or compacts, the kind with two mirrors, one regular and one magnifying. The cheaper the better because you want it to be in a plastic frame that you can break off. Check out the dollar store for a good deal on a super cheap magnifying mirror. Wear safety glasses or goggles in case you break the mirror getting it out, and do it in the garage over some newspaper just in case for easy cleanup. As long as you wear glamour-less safety glasses and set up a safe place to work, you probably won't break the glass—it's kind of like insurance! I found a great shaving mirror at a local big box store in a perfect round black plastic frame that didn't need to be removed, since it was already black and the sharp edges protected, so it really depends on what you find. Once you have the glass free from its frame (or not, as the case may be), use the mirror purifier to clean the entire thing.

Using the nail polish, paint a pentagram on the back and sprinkle with cayenne pepper and black pepper, making sure to get it all along the pentagram. Allow it to dry for ten minutes. Shake off the pepper that isn't stuck to the pentagram. Now apply two coats of black nail polish, covering the entire back of the mirror, allowing it to dry for ten minutes between

Crafting and Enchanting a Witch's Mirror

coats. When you're done, let it dry for about an hour. Now you will stretch the electrical tape around the outside edge of the mirror, pushing down the tape across the front and the back edge of the glass, creating a thin frame around the front and back. Apply attracting mirror wash (chapter 7) to the front of the mirror, and you're ready to go!

To use it, hold the mirror by the edges in your left hand, grasping it where the electrical tape is. Clear everyone but you out of the area. Moving counterclockwise around the house or room you wish to rid of bad vibes, shine the mirror all around, being sure to get the corners of the room or problematic areas in the same way you would use smudge. You can repeat a charm if you like, such as, "Negativity, come right here; take up home inside this mirror." Negativity left from arguments, the evil eye, or even fallout from downright hexes will be sucked into the concave mirror and trapped like they're in a black hole. The electrical tape insulates your fingers from the negative energy, and nothing can get out past the cayenne and black pepper pentagram on the back. Trapped!

When you're done, take it outside, set it in the direct sunlight to burn off the bad vibes, and spritz it with mirror purifier. You can practically see steam rising up and almost hear the Wicked Witch of the West's voice: "I'm melting, melting! Oh, what a world! What a world!"

Seriously, no witches would be harmed, but you can say goodbye to astral nasties. Keep your bad vibe trap mirror wrapped up in black cloth. You may wish to store it next to your attracting mirror wash until the next time you need it.

chapter
7

Mirror Herbal Wash
Formulas and Condensers

Here are some really simple mirror wash formulas that you can use to simultaneously cleanse and enchant your witch's mirrors. My mirror washes are basically herbal infusions mixed with vinegar. Not everyone does it this way, and remember there's no right or wrong way—do what works best for you. So, if you prefer, you may certainly use the formulas as infusion washes without adding vinegar.

That being said, vinegar has long been a magical ingredient for destroying negativity and magical protection, and who can't use both of those attributes? Vinegar can also help your infusion last longer when stored in a spray bottle or corked bottle. Oh, and that vinegary smell? Good news: it disappears magically as soon as it dries! Water and vinegar is the best glass cleaner I've ever found, so these formulas will leave your mirrors squeaky clean and smudge free, with the residual magical vibrations from the herbs and your magical intention.

Before you dig into these formulas, I want to have a brief discussion on the fine art of herb substitutions. I bring this up because I can't tell you how many times I've set out to duplicate an oil, incense, or infusion formula I've found in one of my books, only to discover that I have all except one or two ingredients. Foiled! Or...maybe not. I grab one of my dog-eared, worn-out books on magical herbs and look up the herbs I don't have. What I'm looking for is the magical attributes this particular herb lends to the formula, including magical uses, planetary associations, folklore, etc., and then I look up other herbs with those same attributes. I compare what I find and use the closest match that I have.

This method has never failed to produce good results, and I invite you to do the same if you have a problem finding any of the ingredients in my mirror wash formulas. Keep in mind mirror washes are designed with a specific purpose, such as love, prosperity, healing, or protection, so if you can't find an ingredient easily, it should be simple enough to locate an appropriate substitution or, for that matter, even add an herb of your choice that you like to work with for that magical purpose. Don't ignore what you have in your culinary herb rack and also what you can find in your own backyard. Many of the plants mixed in with your grass that others might call weeds we witches recognize as magical herbs; for example, plantain, dandelions, and clover can all be used as magical herbs. By looking up local native plants, you may be able to double your magical herb stash from your own backyard. As a magical bonus, those plants are magically aligned with the spirits of the land that you walk every day.

I always encourage people to use their creativity—no need to color inside the lines!

To make the infusions in these formulas: Put about a half cup of water into a saucepan and toss in a pinch of each of the herbs the formula calls for (or the appropriate substitutes).

Use a nonmetal or nonreactive saucepan meant for stovetop use such as enamel coated, glass, or pyroceramic glass; these kinds of saucepans won't have any adverse chemical reactions with anything or add molecules of metals into your infusions. I used to use a Pyrex Visions saucepan until it finally broke; now I love my enamel-clad cast iron for making infusions and fluid condensers.

Some people like to reserve a pan just for magical brews; it's a good idea, especially if you're using anything inedible in your washes or condensers. If you're using all nontoxic ingredients it's a matter of personal belief and tradition. Many kitchen witches use the same tools for both magical and culinary purposes, while other traditions prefer to keep mundane and magical tools separate. Be sure to use herbs and not

Mirror Herbal Wash Formulas and Condensers

oils in these formulas. Oils may be used on mirror frames or backs, but generally you don't want your mirror to have an oily, smudgy surface.

Bring the water and herbs to a boil on the stove, then allow to cool. Pour the infusion through a coffee filter that has been secured with a rubber band to the top of a clean glass or jar. Be sure to label it so you don't get it mixed up with your other washes or regular cleaning supplies.

If you want to add vinegar to these mirror wash formulas, simply blend equal amounts of the herbal infusion (after it cools) and white vinegar and put it in a clean spray bottle. If the idea of a plastic spray bottle doesn't appeal to your witchy side, I have a great alternative. If you check the patio, lawn, and garden centers in the spring, you can usually find those really cool old-fashioned glass plant mister bottles. They usually come in a few different colors and have a little metal pump and a really old-world look that is just perfect for applying mirror washes to your magical witch's mirrors! In addition, if you want to get a little fancier with the formulas themselves, you could allow fresh herbs of your choice from the mirror wash recipe to steep in a bottle of vinegar for about a month, and use that vinegar for your mirror washes—pure magic!

Mirror Purifier

Merlin Glass Form

Fluid Condenser

Hexen-Spiegel Wash

New Mirror Purifier

Use this purifier for mirrors that you've purchased new or thrifted. You can also use it to clear old energy from mirrors already existing in your witchy home. This purifier clears away any energies lingering in a mirror so that you have a clean and energetically neutral mirror. Use it for any household mirrors just to clean them, before enchanting them, or for any mirrors you bring home for a magical purpose.

Make an infusion of the following herbs: bay, cedar, chamomile, fennel, lavender, lemon verbena, peppermint, rosemary, sage, thyme, vervain

Use this wash on its own or mix with equal parts plain vinegar or rosemary- or lavender-infused vinegar.

Mercury Glass Wash

If you're creating faux mercury glass as described in chapter 6, you'll need this wash. Also use it to add extra enchantment anytime you feel the need. You can also use this wash to enchant purchased faux mercury glass. If you have found some real antique mercury glass, you can use this wash on a clean cloth to clean and enchant it too, since you're cleaning the glass and not the finish inside its unique double walls.

Make an infusion of the following herbs: violet, lavender, willow, vervain, cinquefoil

Use this wash on its own or mix with equal parts plain vinegar or lavender-infused vinegar.

Protection Mirror Wash

Use this wash for any mirror you want to enchant for protection.

Make an infusion of the following herbs: rue, rowan, cinquefoil, fennel, betony, yarrow

Use this wash on its own or mix with equal parts plain vinegar or fennel-infused vinegar.

Oiel de Sorcière Mirror Wash

Use this wash during the process of constructing a reflective convex mirror that brings a lovely mix of protection and blessings, providing an ever-watchful eye to look out for your home. If you found a new or used oiel de sorcière, this wash is a great way to keep it clean and full of enchantment.

Make an infusion of the following herbs: angelica, St. John's wort, sage, lavender, a bit of iris petal or leaf, eyebright

Use this wash on its own or mix with equal parts plain vinegar or lavender-infused vinegar.

Blessing Mirror Wash

Use this wash on any mirror that you want to use to promote positive energy, uplifting chi, or healing energy. This one is great for house blessings. This is the wash that is called for in the soul fragment retrieval meditation in chapter 9.

Make an infusion of the following herbs: rose petal, angelica, sandalwood, lavender, sage, rosemary

Use this wash on its own or mix with equal parts plain vinegar or rosemary and sage–infused vinegar.

Hexenspiegel Wash

Use this wash to turn any mirror into a protective Hexenspiegel witch's charm that sends out a warning beacon for harmful energies to steer clear of you and will send it right back if the warning is not heeded. Use it for charging your own Hexenspiegel jewelry, suncatchers, or other mirrors you want to charge with the job of sending negative energy that comes your way packing.

Make an infusion of the following herbs: vervain, dill, rosemary, marjoram, holly leaves or berries, rowan, mullein, nettle, agrimony

Use this wash on its own or mix with equal parts plain vinegar or vervain and dill–infused vinegar.

Prosperity Mirror Wash

This is the perfect wash for enchanting a mirror to multiply your prosperity. Use it for making a money-multiplying infinity mirror box, on a mirror in your dining room that reflects your bountiful dinner table, or in your business to reflect your cash register.

Make an infusion of the following herbs: oak leaf, basil, clover leaf or flower, patchouli

Use this wash on its own or mix with equal parts plain vinegar or basil-infused vinegar.

Heart Chakra Mirror Wash

This is great for self-esteem mirrors or mirrors to multiply beauty or love. Use it on your bathroom mirror if you're trying to boost your loving relationship or to heal a broken heart.

Make an infusion of the following herbs: apple peel or leaf, dried rose petals, peppermint, jasmine, geranium, a few drops of honey

Use this wash on its own or mix with equal parts plain vinegar or vinegar infused with sage or marjoram.

Scrying Mirror Wash

Use this wash on your black scrying mirror. This formula vibrates at a high frequency, awakening your third eye so that you can be more open to the visions that you see within the dark, reflective surface.

Make an infusion of the following herbs: eyebright, mugwort, wormwood, vervain

Use this wash on its own or mix with equal parts plain vinegar or vinegar infused with sage or mugwort.

Spirit Communication Wash

Specifically designed for spirit communication, use this one with caution. Be sure to read chapter 6's section on crafting a psychomanteum/spirit communication mirror and chapter 8's psychomanteum spirit contact spell before using this wash. Use this in conjunction with the new mirror purifier, and be a smart witch: never leave such a mirror wide open when not in use.

Make an infusion of the following herbs: mugwort, hawthorn berries or flowers, sweetgrass, wormwood, thistle, sage

Use this wash on its own or mix with equal parts plain vinegar or sage- or mugwort-infused vinegar.

Lunar Mirror Wash

Use for a moon mirror, include boosting magical power and intuition, as well as doubling all the elements and power of any lunar spell.

Make an infusion of the following herbs: willow,
jasmine, white rose petals, moonflower petals or a
seed, mugwort

Use this wash on its own or mix with equal parts plain vinegar, sage- or thyme-infused vinegar, or apple cider vinegar. For extra power add a couple drops of colloidal silver.

Solar Mirror Wash

Use this wash to enchant a sun mirror. A solar-charged mirror can boost success magic and personal power and is great at improving metabolism and communication.

Make an infusion of the following herbs: sunflower,
marigold, cinnamon, St. John's wort, chamomile

Use this wash on its own or mix with equal parts plain vinegar or chamomile-infused vinegar. For extra power add a few drops of colloidal gold.

Attracting Mirror Wash

Use this wash for creating the bad vibe trap in chapter 6. It's also great for invoking or drawing what you want into your life, including money, success, promotions, favors, friendship, or whatever you need more of.

Make an infusion of the following herbs: lovage, calamus root, vervain, lemon verbena, orange zest, rose petal, sandalwood

Use this wash on its own or mix with equal parts plain vinegar or lemon verbena–infused vinegar. Add a small magnet or lodestone to the mix.

Safe Travels Wash for Car Mirrors

While driving have you ever looked in your rearview mirror and used a spur-of-the-moment chant? You know the one: "Slow down, slow down, you're way too close!" The last time I used that chant was during the last month of the time I spent working on this book. The person didn't see me, didn't stop, and I ended up in a five-car pile-up with my mom bumped and bruised and my car totaled. Thankfully no one was killed; it was terrifying.

Here's a mirror wash for safe travels that I devised after that car accident. I'm using it and you can too, dear reader.

I designed this wash to get the attention of those you see in your rearview mirror. If you see them through your rearview mirror that has been enchanted with this wash, they will also see you and pay attention. Keep in mind magic should never be used as a substitute for safe driving habits.

Make an infusion of the following herbs: lemon
zest, feverfew, dandelion, woodbine, elderberries or
elderflowers, 3 drops of Earl Grey tea

Use this wash on its own or mix with equal parts plain vinegar or sage-infused vinegar. Add extra power with a couple drops of colloidal silver.

MIRROR LORE

*A woman who lives alone should carry
a small mirror in her purse to protect
herself from unwelcome company.*

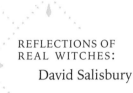

Programming the Witch's Mirror

When I was first learning about magick mirrors, I was only taught one way to program them. Although a cleansing and a dedication are a great way to begin mirror work, I don't see why we have to stop there. As magickal objects, mirrors are like living beings in that they need to be fed and inspired with direction. I like programming my mirror through different potions and powder mixtures to bring about exactly what I need. Using liquid potions, I bathe my mirror or let it soak overnight until it vibrates with the same type of energy as the potion it sits in. I'll do the same with dry herb powders, although sprinkling a little bit over its flat surface is usually good enough. I have even made pastes out of potions and raw herbs combined and smeared that on the mirror's surface in the form of runes and sigils.

One of my favorite washes involves using my mirror for glamour work. Glamour magick isn't always about making yourself seem more attractive. Since I work in politics and advocacy, I use my mirror for glamour magick that helps me give off the type of impression that I want to present myself with to other people. Washing my mirror with oranges and cloves will help me appear successful and fiery. Sprinkling a mixture of lavender and rose petals on my mirror helps me appear more compassionate and approachable. After a good washing, I'll gaze into my mirror and see my reflection morph into the very essence of what I intend to exude in my work.

The results I get after washing a mirror before my work are phenomenal. It makes working with the mirror feel more creative and personal. In addition to the magick brought about by the mirror itself, I'm also aligning myself with the gifts of the elemental powers, which is always helpful when encountering the outside world.

David Salisbury
Author of *Teen Spirit Wicca*,
***The Deep Heart of Witchcraft*,**
and activist and advocate for
human and animal rights •
http://www.daviddsalisbury.com

Mirror Herbal Wash Formulas and Condensers

Mirror Condenser Formulas: It's Electrifying!

Here are a couple of formulas for fluid condensers. I had never attempted to make them myself but had to try it after doing research for this book, and I must say it's a really cool process that produces a potent bottle of powerful magic! As we discussed in chapter 3, washes and condensers are created in a slightly different manner, and washes are designed for specific purposes while condensers are tuned in to more all-encompassing energies—think details versus the big picture. Fluid condensers store power from the spiritual realm in a similar way that an electrical capacitor stores electricity.

Fluid condensers are often associated with mirror magic, but their uses are not limited to mirrors; condensers can be used to anoint other magical items as well, to add blessings and a powerful magical charge. I hope you enjoy learning to make and use condensers as much as I have.

Simple Fluid Condenser for Scrying

A simple fluid condenser contains only one plant; in this case, mugwort. This lunar formula can be used for a scrying mirror or to add lunar power to any mirror. You can make a similar universal fluid condenser using chamomile flowers and colloidal gold instead of the mugwort and colloidal silver called for here. Once you've experimented, you could probably come up with other simple fluid condenser formulas too—just check whether the herb of your choice is aligned with masculine or feminine energies to decide if you should use gold or silver.

Put a half cup of dried mugwort and one cup of water into a small saucepan and bring to a low boil for about twenty minutes. Keep an eye on it, and as you do, visualize the power within the liquid growing.

When the time is up, put the lid on the pot and remove it from the heat. Allow the mixture to cool undisturbed with the lid on. Don't be tempted to peek; just leave it alone—this allows the energies to settle into the liquid. Once it's cool, place a coffee filter into a large Mason jar or coffee cup and secure the top of the filter around the lip of the jar with a rubber band. Pour the liquid through the filter. Now put the strained liquid back into the pan and boil it until the liquid has reduced to about a quarter cup; watch it closely, and don't let it boil dry.

Pour the cooled liquid into a dark colored bottle with a secure stopper and add a quarter cup of vodka, Everclear, or other white alcohol of your choice. Add nine drops of colloidal silver. This fluid will keep and maintain its power for years. Be sure to label it and shake it before every use to activate. It's great for charging your scrying mirror, other witch's mirrors, or crystal balls; you can also use it on many of your magical tools or include it in spellwork.

Mirror Herbal Wash Formulas and Condensers

Solid Scrying Mirror Condenser

This one is a powder and has much more exotic ingredients, but if you're creative you can figure out sources for most of them. Think of the process as part of a hero's quest—the entire process of finding the ingredients adds power to the final product, so no whining. I will offer hints on where you might find some of the more unusual ingredients.

Okay, admit it, these are the kinds of crazy ingredients you always thought would go into a witchy concoction, aren't they?! It's like a metaphysical scavenger hunt, so don't get overwhelmed. Be creative and resourceful, and I bet you can find most of these; you'll only need nine of your choosing. Vegetarians and vegan friends, don't worry, there are plenty of ingredients to choose from so that you can easily create a condenser aligned with your life and magic.

INGREDIENTS

- Dried willow leaves (No willows in your area? Substitute white willow bark herbal supplements.)

- Sea salt (Most grocery stores and metaphysical stores sell sea salt.)

- Powdered oyster shell, crab shell, or lobster shell (Try your grocery store seafood section; just get one claw if you want. Use a metal file to powder the shell. Don't use if you're allergic to shellfish.)

- A feather from a crow, seabird, or waterfowl (Scour rivers, lakes, and beaches; otherwise, look for online sellers with found feathers.)

- Fine filings of a cow bone or stag horn (Beef bones are easy to find; if you prefer stag horn, try ordering stag horn buttons online and obtain powder using a metal file.)

- Dried moss (Life-force in moss is amazingly strong; find moss in parks, on the ground, or on trees.)

- Crushed quartz or amethyst, or both (Don't ruin a good crystal! Just use a small tumbled chip inside a resealable plastic bag and crush it with a hammer.)

- Lichen (This is the stuff that looks like moss but grows on rocks; watch for it in parks or on nature hikes.)

- Crushed olive pit (Eat an olive that was packed in water, dry the pit, and crush it with a hammer.)

- Rosemary (Rosemary is a grocery store staple.)

- Powdered mud dauber wasp nest (Check park pavilions. Be careful and make sure it's an abandoned nest.)

- Cat hair (You can find that on my couch. Seriously: just pet a cat; you'll get hair on your hand. Never

Mirror Herbal Wash Formulas and Condensers

pull out a cat's hair—the gods will be ticked and the cat none too pleased, either. Cut it up as finely as possible with scissors.)

- Dried powdered mushroom (Go for a walk in the woods and be sure to wash your hands; if you can't find one, substitute a grocery store one in a pinch.)

- Powdered eggshell (Grind eggshell to powder in a mortar and pestle.)

- Mugwort (Metaphysical shops carry this herb.)

- Wormwood (You can find this one at metaphysical stores or garden centers.)

- Crushed poppy seeds (Another grocery store herb.)

- Shed snakeskin (This one's tough; if you don't mind appearing strange, a pet shop might help you out.)

- Spider web (I have some in the corners of my house for you; I bet you can find some too.)

- Colloidal silver (Old formulas call for silver extract, but this is the modern way to go. Be sure to make this one of the nine you choose, as it really packs a punch. Find it at your local health food store.)

Now that you've chosen your nine (or, if you're really ambitious, you can use thirteen) of the ingredients above, it's time to make your condenser. You're going to need to make sure that all the ingredients are really pulverized as much as you can. I suggest powdering many of these ingredients separately since they will all present their own challenges. Feathers and cat hair can be cut up into the smallest bits possible with nail scissors. Hard things like shell, horn, and bone can be powdered easily with a metal file. The herbs are easy; a mortar and pestle or a coffee grinder reserved for magical herbs works well. You don't need a lot of each, just a small bit.

Once you have everything powdered, mix it all together in a small jar and add a couple drops of colloidal silver. Now leave the jar open for a few days; the liquid will evaporate out of the colloidal silver, leaving just the silver molecules behind. Once the mixture is completely dry, just break any clumpy bits apart with the back of a spoon. Put the lid on the jar and be sure to label it. When you're ready to make your scrying mirror, after the second coat of paint has been applied, add a very light dusting of the condenser over the paint and allow it to completely dry before applying more paint over the top of it. If you want to use this condenser on a scrying mirror you've purchased, use a clear finish on the back of the mirror and dust the powder on the damp finish. Once the finish is completely dry, add one more coat to seal the condenser within the scrying mirror.

chapter
8

Spells for
Witch's Mirrors

The nervousness that some people hold for the witch's mirror seems to stem from the idea that their only uses are for harmful magic. While that is one use, it's not by any stretch of the imagination the only use. Just like any other witch's tool, the user must constantly work with an awareness of their own ethics and decide the path they want their magic to take. It's important to remember that there isn't a magical tool available that can't be used for either good or harm; the mirror is no exception.

Many people compare the use of magic to the use of electricity and suggest that you can use electricity to light your home and cook your dinner, but it can also kill you and burn your house down, depending on the use. This concept can also apply to the much-maligned witch's mirror. Any witch prepared to put aside old, superstitious ideas about mirrors and get a little creative can come up with many wonderful uses for magical mirrors. As with any magical tool, it's the heart of the witch that's the key to how their magic unfolds.

So how does one come up with spells using mirrors as a magical tool? Mirrors can be used to reflect things, to multiply things you want more of, for magical protection, for blessing a space, for communicating with deity, to boost your energy—the possibilities are endless. This chapter will include some useful spells using mirrors, as well as some magical backing images and seals to help enchant your magical mirrors.

I hope you consider these spells and formulas a jumping-off point and come up with your own ideas for working with witch's mirrors.

MIRROR LORE
In Russia breaking a mirror is believed to cause a rift between you and a close friend or loved one.

House Blessing Witch's Glass Spell

This spell uses a beautiful piece of mercury glass to reflect good intentions and blessings all around your home. You'll need either a real or faux mercury glass jar–type candleholder or hurricane lamp, either storebought or handcrafted (see chapter 6 for instructions). Make sure your mercury glass piece is large enough to set a glass votive holder inside of it. You'll also need a white votive candle anointed with frankincense or sandalwood oil and dropped into a small votive holder. If you're using storebought mercury glass, clean it with chapter 7's new mirror purifier.

Rub some mercury glass wash (see chapter 7) onto the inside and outside of the mercury glass piece to imbue it with energy. As you do, whisper this charm over the glass:

> *Witch's glass I empower*
> *Mirror shine, light divine, shadows cower*

Work with a soft cloth or a paper towel, making sure it's smudge and dust free.

Set the mercury glass in the heart of the home, the place where most of the merriment usually takes place; it's often the kitchen, dining room, or sometimes the family room. Set the candle within the votive holder inside the mercury glass and light it. The first thing you'll notice is that the light radiating out from the mercury glass is twofold: the light from the

175

room is reflected outward by the reflective mercury glass, and the light from the candle within also shines through it, creating a magical and powerful enchantment for your home. Now repeat the enchantment charm again, then carefully take the candle within the mercury glass from one room to the next, repeating the charm in each room of the home and ending back at the heart of the home where you began. Allow the candle to burn out as it simultaneously reflects good vibes and radiates blessings.

The trick is to fill every corner of your life with your own positive intentions until there's no room for baneful energy to fit through your door. Once the initial spell is cast, you may use it for a quick house blessing anytime. Burn votives or tealight candles within the mercury glass from time to time to boost the positive vibrations in the home and cast away negativity.

MIRROR LORE
In some traditions it's bad luck to have two mirrors on the walls directly facing each other in your home.

Mirror Box Wrong Number Spell

This clever spell redirects nasty vibes sent your way from either purposefully negative magic or accidentally cranky people to a magical "wrong number," keeping the negativity away from you.

Yeah, I know—witches don't cause harm, right? Actually, witches are human, and sometimes even if it's not a very nice thing to do, it does happen. Even negative energy from grumpy everyday folks can be unwittingly sent your way. But you can use a box with mirrors on the inside to collect that baneful energy and trap it far away from you.

Obtain a piece of fresh ginger root from the produce section at the grocery store. Using a permanent marker, draw a simple face upon it. Securely wrap the root three times around with copper wire and leave about six inches of wire coming off of the root. Hold the root over your heart and charge it with your intention:

> *Foes think this is me, but it is not*
> *Haters will hate with all they've got*
> *The bane they send addressed to me*
> *Instead this root the receiver shall be*
> *Their target just slightly off its mark*
> *Be it flaming hate or angry spark*

Will only find this precious root
No curse shall find me nor bear fruit
And thus confused their hexes be
Drawn to this root but not to me

Now place the charged root and a couple teaspoons of salt inside the mirrored box. Glue the box closed with a bead of industrial adhesive sprinkled with cayenne and black pepper. When you close the box, make sure the copper wire trails out through the lid with a couple inches outside of the sealed box. The copper wire acts as a spiritual antenna picking up baneful signals sent to you, landing them in your new magical "spam folder," sealed away and never, ever to be opened. Once the energy is drawn in by the ginger root energetically masquerading as you, it becomes trapped by the mirrors in the box and can't escape. The trick is that magical bullies can use up all their energy dialing and sending to a number that's been disconnected, and they won't even know it! (Heh-heh!)

Ideally, this box should be hidden; it can be placed within another box and hidden in an attic, the garage rafters, or buried near the edge of your property, wire side facing away from your home. Should you ever need to get rid of the box, burn it in a bonfire, thus destroying any lingering trapped energy. Another option if you can't do a bonfire is to wrap the whole thing in a brown paper bag and deposit it in a public dumpster at least a mile away from your home.

Return to Sender Spell

Most "return to sender" spells emulate the martial arts concept of letting an attacker's own momentum undo their attack, not only breaking a hex but sending it right back. I used to practice martial arts myself, so I totally get that.

Here's another option for breaking a hex and returning the opposite of what was sent, undoing the bad situation and anger between you and the other person and thus diffusing the situation. Since we'll be using a mirror, we'll reverse it. The benefit of this kind of reversal is that it can put the kibosh on potential "witch wars" that can go on and on, with lightning bolts bouncing back and forth like a tennis match but with no real winners.

If you feel that you've been under attack, first realize that if it's a psychic attack situation, even if you think you know what's happening, you could be wrong. You might be convinced that Endora has been casting against you, but in fact she's been ignoring you completely while Winifred has a poppet that looks just like you that's full of pins. Not nice, sweet Winifred—you didn't see that one coming! The other possibility is that you've been unwittingly "bad-vibing" yourself; yes, it happens. It's easy to get so worked up over an unpleasant interaction with someone that you can actually project your feelings onto the other person and assume they're out to get you. This can cause all kinds of problems that can look just like indicators of a hex, when you are, in fact, manifesting it yourself. I use "anyone not in accord with my greater good" as the name in this spell; that way, if it's someone you don't expect or even yourself, it's all good. The problem will still be solved; after all, isn't that the most important thing?

You'll need a purple taper spell candle, a candleholder appropriate for the candle, and a mirror to set the candle on. Etch a line around the circumference of the candle's middle. From the wick to the center of the candle, rubbing from the wick down, anoint the candle with dragon's blood oil while charging the top half of the candle with the following:

> *I draw all bad vibes into this candle*
> *No matter who sent it, whatever their angle*
> *Anyone not in accord with my greater good*
> *Return it to sender, be it understood*

Now anoint the bottom half of the candle, from the center to the base, with lavender oil, charging the bottom half of the candle with the following:

> *I send it back but flip it around*
> *Reverse it all with magic abound*
> *Reverse thoughts, views, as bad vibes flee*
> *I soothe hard feelings between thee and me*
> *If any shadows have offended*
> *Now turnabout, all discord ended*

Set the candle on the mirror, surround it with a circle of salt, light it, and say:

Reverse, reverse, return to sender
Negative energy must surrender
Opposite, opposite, as I send back
Clear the air and no more flack

Allow it to burn all the way down. The top half of the candle anointed with dragon's blood will draw any negativity from around you and all aspects of your life into the candle. Once the flame reaches the center and the lavender-anointed bottom half, it will reverse the energy to its sender while also reversing the energy itself, healing the situation while at the same time protecting you from future problems.

Smoke and Mirrors Spell

This spell keeps you under the radar when you don't want to be noticed. Bad hair day, you're inundated with work, or you just don't feel like talking to anyone—there are lots of reasons that a witch might want to go unnoticed from time to time.

You'll need a box decorated with mirrors on the outside, a few pumpkin seeds, poppy seeds, and a bit of chicory. You'll also need a printed photo of yourself (on computer paper is fine) and either a sage bundle or a stick of lavender incense.

Light the sage bundle or incense stick and wave your photo through the smoke. Drop the photo inside the box, add the seeds and chicory, fan more smoke inside the box, and slam the box shut, trapping a little smoke inside. Pass the outside of the box through the smoke; as you do, repeat this charm:

> *Smoke and mirrors work for me*
> *Grant me invisibility*
> *I journey quietly through my day*
> *Unwanted attention stay away*
> *Safe, shielded, blessed, and obscured*
> *With harm to none, this spell's secured*

The last two lines of the charm are meant to keep you from being accidentally bumped into, unnoticed at a busy intersection, or anytime going unseen wouldn't be safe. Leave the box on a shelf, table, or altar where it will be undisturbed, and go about your day unbothered. The spell creates a camouflage effect; you won't literally be invisible, so you can't sneak up and tie anyone's shoelaces together, but you will simply be unnoticed.

When you're ready to break the spell (don't forget about it or you'll be wondering why everyone is ignoring you), open the box and say:

> *Invisibility is now undone*
> *Cast smoke and mirrors to the sun!*

Chapter 8

Take everything out; leave the seeds and chicory as an offering somewhere in nature. Leave the photo in a sunny window to shine away the enchantment, and leave the open box in the sunshine for at least one hour.

Psychomanteum Spirit Contact Spell

With this spell you can safely open a portal to the other side of the veil to contact loved ones. You can also use this spell to contact familiar spirits, spirit guides, or even your patron deity. Use either a black scrying mirror or silver mirror; this special mirror can be constructed with the instructions in chapter 6. If looking into mirrors in a dark room or using a spirit board oracle such as a Ouija board freaks you out, you may want to pass this one by.

Set up your room. A traditional psychomanteum was a small booth all draped in black, with nothing but a large mirror and a chair, but you don't have to go that far to get good results. Set up in a quiet room, play music that was appreciated by the person or spirit you want to contact, and angle the mirror so that it reflects the room but does not capture your own reflection. You may instead wish to hang a black cloak in such a way that it is the only thing seen within the reflection from the angle of your chair. Place a photo and/or items owned by or significant to the person you wish to contact. If you're contacting a spirit guide or deity, use items that you associate with them or pictures that represent them. Turn off the lights and have either a very dim light or a candle somewhere behind you, safely away from anything flammable. Soften your gaze into the mirror and repeat the following evocation to open communication:

Harken ye spirits of the next world
This portal of aether is unfurled
As I reach out to thee across the abyss
We share kind thoughts from your world to this
Any spirits whose motives aren't pure
Shan't cross this gate, my magic secure
Those who commune for my greatest good
Our thoughts and words shall be understood

Communication may come in the form of visions, a voice, or even feelings. You may or may not physically see the person, but you might sense their presence in other ways. If at any point you feel uncomfortable or are afraid, spray the mirror with purifier and declare firmly, "I close this portal now," to shut it down right away. Once you have reached the end of your spirit communication session, announce the following devocation and commence closing the mirror:

Harken ye spirits, our visit is finishing
This portal of aether now is diminishing
Return to your realm and light the way

Harming none along the way
I thank you sincerely and honor your time
Gratitude for communion from your world to mine

At this point you may turn on the light and cleanse the front of the mirror with mirror purifier to close the portal, which is like hanging up the phone at the end of a conversation.

Sun Mirror Metabolism Booster Spell

Have you ever had that feeling that your energy is low, you're worn out, and you can't seem to jumpstart yourself? Does brain fog take over so much that even an extra cup of coffee just leaves your hands shaky but not energized? When I reached fifty years in this body, I found that my metabolism wasn't the same as it once was, so I invented this method for a metabolism booster. (Even you young witches might like it too.) The stresses of daily life, being overworked, or not getting enough sleep at night can all be contributing factors to low energy. As a witch and a human being, we need that energy to manifest our goals, so let's take it back!

Our energy system is made up of chakras. Chakras are energy centers located in the body that correspond to locations in your spirit or astral body that act as conduits or connectors between you and the spirit of everything. The chakra that is the core of our personal power is called the solar

185

plexus chakra. It's a vortex of energy located between your belly button and the bottom of your sternum, and it's the center of willpower, self-esteem, and joy. This important energy center can get blocked and sludged up with self-doubt, shame, and lack of confidence, making you feel like all you can do is sit passively and watch life go by. Oh, heck no—we'll have none of that! I've got a mirror magic fix to help you get your solar plexus chakra clean and healthy so you start running your life again, boosting your metabolism, personal energy, and self-confidence.

All you need for this spell is a sun mirror made from a flat mirror (don't use convex or concave; see instructions for making one in chapter 6), a sunny day, and your powers of visualization. First locate your solar plexus chakra: feel under your rib cage for your sternum, the flexible bone that holds your ribs together in the front. Move your fingers down the center of your chest to the very bottom point of your sternum. Now put the fingers of your other hand on your belly button and find the spot that's right between the two; that's where your solar plexus chakra is. Step outside on a sunny day with your sun mirror—noon may work best—and find a position where you can stand or sit and still reflect the rays from the mirror onto the center of your solar plexus chakra. This may take a little bit of trial and error; it's best if the sun is over one shoulder. Be careful not to shoot yourself right in the eye with the sun's rays. Once you've got it, let it linger there on your solar plexus, shining its light.

Allow the power of the sun to fill your solar plexus with its power; as you do, visualize a glowing yellow light there. Visualize the light of the sun reflected in the sun mirror beginning to burn away dark-colored blockages within the chakra; like light blasting away shadows, any psychic sludge within the chakra fades away and your solar plexus brims with yellow light. See the light spinning, pulsing, and glowing as it begins to morph into a brilliant yellow lotus flower. Keep the sun mirror shining on your solar plexus as long as you wish, and soak up those good rays. Once you're done, you will start to feel energy return into your body and life. Drink lots of water over the next several days in order to help your body release any toxins that have built up.

MIRROR LORE
In Russia it's believed that
if you eat in front of a mirror,
it will ruin your good looks.

Mirrored Orb Garden Prosperity Spell

Why not have a witch's mirror in the garden? My favorite witch's garden mirror is a reflective gazing ball. These first became popular during Victorian times but have enjoyed a resurgence over the last decade as a beautiful garden ornament. Additionally, they are delightful for working magic in the garden.

Your garden is a symbol of your abundance and prosperity—everything green and growing, celebrating the cycles of life right in your own yard. A gazing ball reflects and multiplies that abundance of growth, creating what looks like a little microcosm of plenty while magically creating more prosperity in your life.

Because this kind of mirror stays outside, I like to charge it using my will, words, crystals, and plants because a mirror wash can disappear with the next rainstorm. You'll need a reflective gazing ball with a base, a compass (or, for techie witches, a compass app on your phone), a small citrine tumbled stone, and four plants of your choice for prosperity, such as basil, mint, or marigolds. Find a perfect spot in your garden for the gazing ball and poke the little citrine crystal right under the base and into the ground. Now plant your prosperity plants right around the base, one at each of the cardinal points (east, south, west, and north).

Grab a cloth and wipe the gazing ball and base clean all around as you say:

Orb of magic, shining bright
Multiply abundance within my sight
Air, fire, water, and earth
I'm open to life and all it's worth
Boost my prosperous energy
By my true will, so mote it be

Now your lovely witch's garden mirror will not only look beautiful as a focal point in your garden, but it will open the way to increased prosperity in your life!

MIRROR LORE
In India looking in a mirror that's
already broken is bad luck.

Multiply My Fortunes Infinity Box Spell

Here's a quick and easy mirrored box prosperity spell. It's perfect for when you're trying to make rent or have some extra unexpected expenses pop up. Check chapter 6 for details on how to make a mirrored box. For this box, you'll want a box mirrored on the inside in the style of the infinity mirror: two mirrors directly across from each other inside the box.

Once you have your box with two mirrors inside, you'll notice that anything you put inside the box is reflected in both mirrors, repeated over and over into infinity. (See where I'm going with this?) Money is just energy, and there is enough energy in the universe for everyone. This spell manifests that concept into your reality.

Take the largest bill you can spare—even a dollar is fine. Wrap an acorn in the bill, twisting it at the ends like a piece of hard candy. Place it inside the box and speak these words into the box:

> *I multiply this seed I sow*
> *It grows into infinity*
> *As all my riches grow and grow*
> *I welcome in prosperity*

Close the box and leave it be. Watch for ideas and opportunities to access the money you need. A bag of money won't land on your doorstep (probably), but people who owe you

Compact mirror healing spell setup

will probably repay you, you'll get a great idea to earn some extra cash, or an offer to earn more money—a promotion, a raise, or a side job—will come your way shortly. Keep an eye out for all opportunities; your prosperity is being repeated into infinity.

Shining Compact Mirror Healing Spell

A mirror can be a boost for any type of candle spell. Back in the days before electric lights, there were many candle lanterns and wall sconces designed as shiny reflectors to multiply the candles' light. I think they might have been on to something. If a mirror can multiply a candle's flame, why not use it to multiply the magical energy as well? Let's employ some simple mirror magic to multiply your magical efforts—in this instance, a healing spell.

Say that someone has asked you to send them healing energy; with social media and more acceptance and understanding about the witch's path, it's a more common occurrence all the time. As a Reiki Master/teacher, I get healing requests all the time. Sometimes I just send Reiki, but sometimes I like to Reiki charge a candle and add my witchy touch, depending on the person I'm doing healing for and what they would prefer. It should also be said here to use healing magic with common sense and in addition to medical care, never instead of it.

Grab a tealight candle in the color you like to use for healing—purple, blue, or green (white is a great all-purpose go-to color). Lift the candle out of the holder. Write the name of your friend in need of healing on a small slip of paper, fold it, and place it underneath the candle within the metal tealight cup. You can carve their name into the top using a crystal point or a pencil, then anoint the candle with an oil for healing such as sandalwood, rosemary, or your favorite healing blend. If you wish, give it a sprinkle of healing herbs, such as cinnamon or ground rose petals.

Now place a simple two-sided compact mirror on your altar. Open it with the magnifying side (if there is one) flat on your altar or workspace, reflecting the ceiling, and the other side at a 90-degree angle. Set your tealight on top of the mirror and surround it with stones for healing, such as quartz, moonstone, or rose quartz. I always use a small piece of peacock ore when sending healing energy. Including a statue of your favorite healing deity and a photo of your friend or a gift they gave you can be a nice touch and a good way to align with their energy. To charge your candle, say:

> *By the power of mirrors and witch's flame*
> *I send forth healing for (insert name) to claim*
> *I see (him/her) healed in my mind's eye*
> *May it manifest as these powers do fly!*

The mirror will increase the power of the healing spell by reflecting and duplicating it. The mirror beneath the candle draws healing energy into the spiritual realm; the one next to the candle at a 90-degree angle multiplies all energy sent into the material plane. Now you have activated the axiom "as above, so below," working its powerful truth as healing energy zips off to help your friend in need.

If you ask me, that's some powerfully positive mirror magic! What kind of candle magic could you think of to boost with the help of a witch's mirror?

Indian Toran Doorway or Window Spell

These brightly colored embroidered door hangings sparkling with tiny mirrors lend a lovely exotic air to your home. I ended up hanging several in my bedroom when I redecorated with an Indian/gypsy flair, using them for doors and as window treatments. They really add a lovely energy to the space.

As I discovered much to my delight, the lovely shisha mirror work they are covered with is meant to fill the home with magical blessings and fertility while deflecting the evil eye. While I'm no longer interested in literal fertility myself, a fertile harvest, a fertile imagination—that's for me. However, if you are trying to conceive a baby, a toran might be just what you need; heck, it sure can't hurt! Here's how to enchant a decorative toran doorway hanging to keep the evil eye away and bestow blessings of good fortune.

These beautiful hangings are created with intent in mind. All you really need to do is clear it and program it with your magical intention. Once you have your toran, hang it up with clothespins (office clips work too) somewhere outside where the wind can blow over it and the sun can shine upon its mirrors. The sun is important to magically activating your toran; it was believed that the mirrors would reflect the desert sun around a room to blast away negativity from the space. You can leave it there for a couple hours; that should be plenty. When you take it down, give it a good shake and bring it inside. Hang it right away over a door or window of your choice. After you have it right where you want it, hold the palms of your hands over the fabric and allow it to be filled with your positive intentions. Visualize the tiny mirrors reflecting love, joy, peace, protection, and blessings all over the room. Then seal it with these words or something similar:

> *Blessed toran, shisha shine*
> *Pour your blessings on me and mine*
> *Shine away darkness from this place*
> *Transform it into sacred space*

Now your toran will do its duty: looking beautiful, bestowing blessings, and deflecting the evil eye. It will give your special room and home a feeling of being a wonderful sanctuary.

You Are Beautiful Spell

You are a beautiful person. You are! We all need a reminder from time to time. Sometimes it's easy to get so wrapped up in crazy concepts like "ideal beauty" or the perfect images we see in magazines, which aren't real anyway. My mom used to do photoshop touch-ups for magazines; I've seen the "before" photos, and no one actually looks like what you see in the magazines, not even the people in the photos. With all that input it's hard to remember that the light that radiates out of us is so much more powerful than our jeans size, complexion, or laugh lines. What other people see is often not what we see because we pick ourselves apart for our tiny "flaws," the same ones that other people actually find beautiful or endearing. We're going to change all that with a wonderful mirror spell to remind you every day that you are totally beautiful while you draw your inner light outward for everyone to see. This spell uses your own bathroom mirror—the one you look into every single day.

First, use the mirror purifier to get rid of the lingering energy from every single morning when you looked in the mirror and then gave yourself a hard time for not being a touched-up supermodel or pumped-up athlete. Clear it all away! Begone!

Now use chapter 7's heart chakra mirror wash to amp up loving vibrations; it's time to start seeing yourself through loving eyes. Grab a sheet of paper and divide it into ten slips about the size of business cards. Now comes the moment of truth, and I mean it. You are to write yourself ten compliments on those slips of paper, and I mean raving compliments that all begin with "you are beautiful." They can be physical, such as "You are beautiful, and you have sparkling, warm eyes," or completely spirit-oriented, such as "You are beautiful and always help other people out when they need it." Ideally, they should be half physical and half spiritual. When you are done, stand before the mirror and hold the first compliment, pressing it with the words facing the reflection against the mirror, while looking yourself right in the eye. Say:

Blessed mirror, help me see
The truth of beauty inside of me

Fold it in half and drop it into a pretty jar or box. Repeat with each slip until they're all inside your container. Keep it either tucked inside your medicine cabinet or on your vanity. Every morning when you see yourself in the mirror, randomly choose one slip from the jar or box and speak it out loud several times. Gaze deeply into your own eyes in the mirror and remind yourself that it's true. You're not allowed to add any disclaimers during this short ritual, like "…but your fingernails are a mess." Only the positive, loving statement is allowed.

It will seem strange at first. We're programmed to believe that being self-deprecating is noble and that appreciating yourself is vain, but these are outdated, guilt-based concepts that only serve to tether and bind your true spirit. You are a witch with the power of the universe inside of you. You have the right to feel joy and allow the reflection of the powerful witch that you are to give you a daily reminder of your inner and outer beauty. Go forth, and keep being awesome!

Magic for the Young Witch

Before delving into this next spell, let's think about the ways that teens, tweens, and even younger kids pay more attention to what they see in the mirror than we might realize. If the kids you know seem to be obsessed with their appearance, it might not be vanity—it might just be insecurity that they don't see what society tells them is acceptable in that mirror.

Growing up can be a hard time of life. Lots of young people feel like they are under more and more pressure to live up to other people's standards, which are often also completely unrealistic standards. As well, kids are bombarded with all kinds of marketing images and social propaganda that can often leave them feeling like they just can't live up to what they think the world expects of them. The current media version of the ideal for women is achievable by about 5 percent of women at most; let's face it, lumps and bumps are photoshopped out, legs are made longer, nothing you see in magazines is even remotely real—even supermodels don't actually look like their photos. Boys can have a hard time too. Although statistically more girls have body image issues, don't ignore the fact that some boys feel the same way and may also need a boost of self-esteem to get them through the awkward years.

The truth is, sometimes mirrors lie—well, to be fair, it's not the mirror that's lying, it's how our brain interprets that image in the mirror. When we focus on only what we believe are flaws, they seem more prominent because our brain focuses on that, not allowing us to see the beautiful parts of our reflection. Silly brain, knock it off!

One of the factors in how we see ourselves in the mirror is mood. Research shows that when we're happy, we find ourselves more attractive than when we're feeling low. Kids are under so much pressure that even at a young age they sometimes need some extra help getting through the time in their lives when mirror image and actual appearance can be so different. Here's a really fun project to help a young witch create their own witch's mirror to give them a little boost of self-esteem just when they need it the most.

A Young Witch's Self-Esteem Mirror Spell

This mirror magically melds the daily growing and changing image of an important kid in your life with positive energy created with love, reflecting their personality, positive attributes, and radiating love every day. The most important part of this project is not how perfect it is or how artistically balanced; the key to this project is that you make it fun, happy, and empowering. Make sure the recipient of the mirror gets creative input so that when they're done they can be proud of it, and every time they look into it they will feel the love radiating from this mirror that went into making it. In other words, no one gets in trouble if they don't "color inside the lines."

SUPPLIES

- A mirror in a frame (Make sure it's at least big enough for head and shoulders, sixteen by twenty inches or a full-length mirror is fine too.)

- Heart chakra mirror wash from chapter 7.

- St. John's wort (Just grab a small bottle of St. John's wort supplements from the pharmacy; you'll need half the powder from inside a capsule.)

- Paint for the frame (Pick out a color of paint that your young person likes, their favorite color that makes them feel confident. I like a water-based

GREAT SMILE · Loyal friend · Science Wiz · Honest · AMAZING & Singing voice · Beautiful EYES · Helper of Animals · Hair like Chocolate · CUTE TOES · GREAT FRIEND · TICKET · Cool Style · LOVE DANCING! · KIND

A self-esteem mirror spell

gloss enamel, which you can find in little bottles at your local craft store. Look for a one-step self-sealing paint.)

- A few paint pens (Choose more of your young witch's favorite colors. Make sure you get ones that say they work on glass.)

- Items from the heart (Small rose quartz or clear crystal, the young person's birthstone, a seashell from a family trip, a ticket from the school play they were in; keep it symbolic—think keepsakes.)

- Hot glue gun

Spray some heart chakra mirror wash onto the mirror to charge it up with loving vibrations. Open one St. John's wort capsule and empty about half of it right into the paint and stir or shake it up really well. St. John's wort is a very cheery herb that lifts moods. We have some growing wild around here, it makes you smile just to see it. The dried herb holds all that power.

Lay down newspaper or a large sheet of plastic to protect your work surface. Put on this kid's favorite music or movie that always makes them smile while you work together (I bet your young witch would love to help). Using soft brushes, cover the frame with the paint. It might take a couple of coats. Be as neat as you can, but don't freak out if a little paint gets on the glass; you can scrape it off with a razor when you're done. Once the paint is dry, now comes the fun part.

While the paint dries, sit down together and make a list on a separate sheet of paper of all the wonderful things about this amazing young person. Write down everything that makes this kid beautiful: "great smile, sings like a bird, excellent shortstop, totally funny, pretty red hair, great fashion sense, gazes at the stars, cute toes, warm brown eyes"—write it all down.

Here's a tip: if there's a physical attribute they don't like, ask yourself if there's a celebrity with the same attribute. When I was in high school, I felt like my shoulders were too wide. Yep, that's a randomly ridiculous thing for a young lady to worry about, but there you go. My brilliant mom pointed out that Marilyn Monroe didn't have narrow little shoulders, just look at her in that famous halter dress! Oh, wow…revelation! Suddenly I liked my shoulders just fine; in fact, I thought they were very cool. So my mirror would have included the phrase "Marilyn Monroe shoulders." If your kid has a mole like Cindy Crawford, a smile like Anna Paquin, or hair like David Tenant, why not point out that a celebrity that's considered quite awesome and attractive has that same attribute! It turns what they've perceived in the mirror as a negative into a big ol' positive.

Now, using the paint pens, write these fabulous phrases all over the frame. You can even let them trail over from the frame onto the edges of the glass, but no more than an inch or so—keep the rest of the mirror open so that lovely kid can see themselves surrounded by positive phrases. Add swirl shapes, moons and stars, hearts, spirals, anything at all.

Next, you can hot glue some special items with positive memories or connections to the frame. You can put them all in a pattern in one or two corners or space them out all over the frame. Watch fingers while using hot glue, especially if you're making a mirror with a young child. Teens and tweens might actually enjoy being able to glue these items on themselves. These magical talismans of happiness will add extra power to the mirror. Once you're finished, write a special message on the back of the mirror from you to your young witch to let them know that they are loved, special, and perfect just the way they are, then sign it.

Help your young mirror-making partner find a good place to hang the mirror in their room, making sure that it's the right height not to cut off the top of their head. Put it in a good spot where they can use it every day while getting ready. With a little magic and a lot of love, the mirror should reflect a more accurate image of this wonderful young witch as they grow into their ability to face the world with confidence.

Spells for Witch's Mirrors

REFLECTIONS OF
REAL WITCHES:
Michael Furie

Manifesting Magical Goals

A versatile technique to help manifest magical goals is the use of a regular silver-backed mirror. Since one of the things the mirror can symbolize is the astral realm where magic can begin, I like to place a mirror on (or in front of) my altar and have a symbol of my magical goal reflected into the glass in order to add another dimension to the magic. If I'm working for something tangible like a new home, a vehicle, etc., a photograph or model of the type of item I desire can be placed so that it can only be seen in the mirror (thus existing in the astral), then energy can be sent through a wand, athame, or pointing finger into the mirror's reflection.

Afterward, the symbol or photograph can be turned so that it is not reflected in the mirror, thereby claiming it in physical reality. When the item is turned so that it becomes a part of this world, it affirms that our magic is working to manifest our goal in reality and also that the energy has progressed from our spell into the astral realm, then back down into the physical world. The symbol then becomes a type of charm helping to attract the goal in addition to whatever spell was used as the primary magic. Though a special mirror dedicated only to magic would be ideal for this type of work, any mirror can be used. A vanity table with an attached mirror could be an altar table, and in a pinch a makeshift altar could even be set up in front of the bathroom mirror.

This method can be used as an accompaniment to almost any other magic. As an example, in a candle spell, having the candles reflected in the mirror along with the symbol enhances the energy and atmosphere of the working without having to become the main focus (unless desired). If making a cord or charm as the main spell, having a symbol reflected in the mirror provides a mental focus to concentrate upon in order to keep the magical goal firmly in the forefront of the mind while completing the charm. No matter what magical process is used, adding the aspect of mirror work to it can provide enhancement to an already established practice, potentially adding new layers of depth and energy to the spell.

Michael Furie
Author of *Supermarket Magic*
and *Spellcasting for Beginners* •
www.michaelfurie.com

207

Spells for Witch's Mirrors

Backing Images and Magical Seals

Backing images have been used in magical mirrors since the times of the Romans and Egyptians. Most mirrors back then were hand mirrors and were often highly decorated with symbols and images of deities. A mirror with a goddess on the back might help the user to invoke the power of the goddess's beauty or talents.

A backing image is a great way to add special powers and attributes to your witch's mirror. It can either be added as a visible decoration like you might see adorning a pretty compact mirror or hand mirror, or it can also be a design that's hidden, placed inside the frame facing the back of the mirror or painted on the back of the mirror. A backing image symbolically adds programming to your mirror. You can add a backing image to any kind of witch's mirror you wish.

Whether the image shows or is hidden does not affect the power it attaches to the mirror, so it's really just a matter of taste. As an artist I really like to add imagery to my magic, but you don't have to be artistically inclined to add a backing image to your witch's mirror. Some symbols are easy to draw and skill level doesn't affect the power involved. Often pentagrams, Viking runes, hieroglyphs, and even some of the simpler magical seals can be reproduced fairly easily. Printouts of many of these types of designs would be easy to trace yourself by taping it to the back of a sheet of printer paper and using a window as a makeshift light table to easily see through the paper. Use light pencil lines to trace the image, then you can go over it with any pen you like or even a nib with magical ink such as dragon's blood ink. By drawing it yourself, you add extra personal energy to the project. After you have the image copied onto a piece of paper, you can apply the sheet of paper to the back of the mirror by simply using tape, a glue stick, or decoupage medium.

If you would like to add a permanent painted sigil backing image, I have an easy way to add a simple black-and-white design using a pencil, thin-tip permanent marker, and a piece of thin tissue paper like the kind you put in gift bags (find it in the greeting card/gift wrap aisle). Lay a piece of thin white tissue paper on top of the image you want to reproduce. Tape it in place using blue painter's masking tape, which can be found in any store that carries house paint; it's low tack and won't damage the original that you're tracing it from. Trace the design using a pencil and, being careful not to tear the tissue paper, take the traced art and securely tape it to the back of the mirror. Now you'll need a brand-new thin-point permanent marker. Using the marker, trace the design carefully, making sure not to move the art as you work. When you're done, remove the tissue paper; you'll find that the outline of the design has bled through the tissue paper onto the mirror back. Now you can either go over it with the permanent

Spells for Witch's Mirrors

marker again to clean up the lines or you can use a paint pen meant for use on glass. Any mistakes with the permanent marker can be removed gently with hairspray on a cotton swab once the paint is completely dry.

For more complex images like deities, you can often find copyright-free images online to print out and use as is by using tape, glue, or decoupage medium to affix them to the back of your mirror. Just watch to make sure they're in public domain, which doesn't mean it was found on the Internet; it means the artist who created it is either no longer alive and no one else retains the rights or that the artist has specifically offered the work for free to people who want to use it. If you're in doubt of the source, you can drag the image into an image search bar on your search engine, and that will usually identify the original source easily. Wise witches never use art without permission anymore than they would use a five-finger discount to gather any other magical supplies like incense, crystals, or candles. Making magic with hijacked or stolen supplies is a good way to have your magic backfire or offend the very deity you want to work with, and that's never a good idea. If in doubt, look for images of deities found on archaeological items. These should not be infringing on any copyrights since the creators of the images are history, literally—plus these images have a powerful connection to the historical worship of that deity.

I've included some symbols of my own design that would make great backing images for witch's mirrors. You are free to use them for your personal mirrors. I hope you find these useful and that they inspire you to come up with more of your own.

Mirror of the Moon
(love, healing, intuition)

Mirror of the Sun
(prosperity, joy, growth)

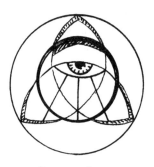

Oeil de Sorcière
(protection and blessings)

Hexenspiegel Seal
(protection, wards
against evil eye)

Hulinhjalmur
(invisibility)

Spirit Portal Sigil: Psychomanteum
(safely guarded spirit gate)

chapter
9

Mirror Meditations:
Betwixt and Between the Worlds

Witch's mirrors are a wonderful meditation tool. Witches walk between the worlds, so what better way to practice some great magical meditations than with a gateway between the worlds? A mirror gives us an opportunity to see everything with a new perspective, look inside ourselves, and explore the astral realm.

Before we delve into meditations using mirrors, let's gain some insight into the significance of how the human mind and a few very elite animal minds perceive the abstract concept of the common mirror.

Mirror Self-Recognition and
Its Significance in Magic

How old were you when you knew that was your own reflection in the mirror and not just another baby? I'm sure you don't remember—I sure don't—but researchers have discovered that humans have the ability for self-recognition in a mirror at about fifteen to eighteen months old. This pivotal stage of psychological development is called the "mirror stage" (no big surprise there). But it's actually a big turning point in the development of our psyches, and our mind is our most important magical tool. The realization that the person in the mirror is actually you is something we all take for granted, but it points to an ability to understand the symbolic and the abstract. The ability to recognize that a mirror is a reflection also points to the realization of the relationship between the ego and the physical body.

Why is this significant? It seems like anyone who has eyes would know what a mirror is, right? Actually, there are only a few select animals that we know of with the ability to recognize that a mirror is not another animal but is, in fact, themselves. It takes some special higher brain functions to understand the symbolic nature of a reflection.

Interestingly, mammals seem to have an advantage in mirror recognition skills, but even then, very few of them can do it. In 1970 psychologist Gordon Gallup Jr. used similar tests as the ones used to discover the mirror stage in human children in order to determine whether other members of the animal kingdom had the ability for mirror self-recognition, which is an indicator for abstract thought and symbol recognition. A mark is placed on the animal and then they're shown their own reflection; if the animal reacts to the mark on their own body when they see it in the reflection, this is a sign that they are recognizing themselves and grasping an abstract idea—the mirror as a symbol of themselves.

Among the stars of his experiments were members of the great apes, Asian elephants, bottlenose dolphins, and a non-mammal, the Eurasian magpie. (I knew I liked those magpies; we both like to collect pretty sparklies! Interestingly, in Russian folklore magpies are heavily associated with witches; that might not be a coincidence.) That's not a lot of animals to have high marks in mirror self-recognition.

There are more animals that tested marginally well, such as pigs, ravens, and crows. In a recent study New Caledonian crows were able to use mirrors to locate food in a mazelike cage, thus showing an understanding of the properties of mirrors. There are lots of anecdotal stories about other animal species likely displaying symbolic thought and understandings of mirrors, but among them were not cats or dogs, which we consider to be very intelligent. Dogs and cats are less visual and more likely to recognize by smell or hearing, so although they probably don't think the mirror is another dog or cat, they don't generally seem to think it's themselves either, as far as we can tell. Tests using senses other than sight can prove dog and cat intelligence and self-awareness (which we all knew anyway), but that's still different than the abstract thought it takes to understand mirrors. Your dog doesn't give a fig about a photo of a steak, but many humans will actually get hungry looking at that photo.

The ability to self-recognize in a mirror is not a test of intelligence per se but is more a test of imagination and symbolic thinking. The animal species that passed are also species that are considered to be highly intelligent, but additionally most of them have shown an understanding of symbols. One of many examples is the interesting case of Kanzi, a bonobo that learned to communicate through the use of more than two hundred symbols on a keyboard. The ability to recognize symbols and an abstract idea like a mirror is actually a pretty big deal.

If you think about it, an important part of magic is the use of symbols. In the craft of the witch we use symbolic candle colors, god and goddess images, runes and sigils; think of all the magical correspondences that make up your magical practice. The very concept of a spell is that one thing can represent another thing and that they can be linked. The ability to recognize your reflection points to a human's ability for understanding abstract thought and the significance of symbols, which is what's necessary for shamanic journeying, meditation, and pretty much every form of magic. Without the ability for a species to reach the developmental stage known as the "mirror stage," could we even practice witchcraft at all?

Now it's time to let that amazing abstract-thinking brain of yours out to play. Enjoy contemplating the complexity of the symbol of the mirror while you discover some witchy ways to use it as a tool for deeper self-discovery. Here are a few mirror meditations for you to try. Will you travel to other realms, heal your soul, or awaken your ability to see the unseen? Leave your inhibitions behind and join me on the other side of the mirror.

MIRROR LORE

Why does a broken mirror
traditionally bring seven years of
bad luck? That's the period of time
that the ancient Romans believed it
took for the soul to renew itself.

Astral Travel Through the Looking Glass

There are many methods for traveling into the astral realm; here's one using a mirror. Many people like to use out-of-body experiences to explore aspects of the spirit realm or even faraway places in the physical world. Astral travel requires you to visualize yourself outside and beyond your physical body; how better to do that while looking at your own reflection that seems to be you but is not you? If that makes sense to you, mirrors might be a great method for exploring the art of astral travel.

Don't be disappointed if you can't accomplish astral travel the first time you try it. Most people have to practice the process; the more you do it, the easier it will become. The trick is trying not to try, which is harder than it sounds. I think sci-fi/fantasy humorist Douglas Adams nailed it when he wrote, "The knack of flying is learning how to throw yourself at the ground and miss."

Some people prefer a completely quiet room. I personally like some very quiet relaxing instrumental music and a stick of my favorite incense, but it's really a matter of whatever helps you relax and reach a meditative state.

First, decide what your goal will be. Even if it's just to experiment with astral travel, that's still a goal. Sit comfortably with your entire body's reflection in a full-length mirror. Take in the reflection, taking note of every little detail—folds in your clothing, the shape of your arms, strands of hair; every single detail. Notice how the light highlights parts of the image and shadows create contrast elsewhere. Look at your reflection in a completely objective way, analyzing shapes and colors, light and dark. Take as long as you need. Once you feel that you have every detail memorized to the point where you could paint it or describe every detail, close your eyes.

Once your eyes are closed, re-create that image of yourself in your mind's eye, pulling all those details into the image until you've re-created a living image of yourself. Once you feel the image in your mind is solid—every detail in place, just the way you remember it—using only your mind and not your physical body, imagine yourself raising your arm and watching in your mind's eye the mirror image do the same. With your eyes still closed, repeat this process, raising the other arm, wiggling your fingers, tipping your head from side to side. Once you feel that you have this game of "mirror image" with yourself down, you're ready to move to the next step.

Now shift your consciousness into your mirror image. Do you walk across the room and sit down within your nonphysical body? Do you fly across the room into your doppelganger? Do you just focus your attention on it and make a smooth transition from your physical body to your astral body? Many people will find that different things work better for them than others. There's no right or wrong way to do it; just find a way that works for you. Once you feel your consciousness settle within the astral body, with your physical eyes still closed, open your astral eyes and look out through the eyes of your "spirit self."

Now move your spirit arm and wiggle your fingers in front of your face. Look around the room—you can even get up and move around the room if you wish. Recall the goal you decided on in the beginning of the exercise. If you just wanted to focus on practice, move around a bit and see what you can do in your nonphysical body. Do you want to levitate? Interact with objects in your surroundings: will an object into existence, put your hand through the wall. If you set a goal for visiting a different physical reality or higher plane, now is the time to do that. What will you experience, what will you see? Complete your mission.

Once you are ready, allow your consciousness to return to your physical body. Feel your being begin to fill up the space that is your body, stretching your consciousness into yourself like a hand into a glove. Feel the breath fill your lungs, the sensations of the physical returning. Take your time, and when you're ready, slowly open your eyes. You may want to take some time sitting quietly in the physical world before fully jumping back into daily tasks, just as you take your time waking up in the morning.

You may want to practice this technique and keep track of your progress in a journal. Don't be frustrated if it takes time to master the technique—nothing worthwhile ever came easy—and keep in mind how long it took when you were just a baby to learn how to walk around in your physical body. With time and practice you can use this technique to assist in self-healing, spiritual development, exploration of the realms of spirit, and much more; the only limit is your own imagination, so let it soar.

REFLECTIONS OF
REAL WITCHES:
Raven Digitalis

Mirrors as Magickal Amplifiers and Otherworldly Portals

Mirrors are such a fascinating topic when it comes to folklore, magick, and metaphysics. Through the expanse of human history we have been seeking our reflections in various ways and for various reasons. Rich folklore exists surrounding mirrors and similarly reflective objects. Mirrors have been both loved and feared for centuries.

Bodies of water are the most mirrorlike surfaces available in the natural world. For obvious reasons, mirrors of all types find an elemental alignment with Water in numerous magickal and metaphysical philosophies. At my own multicultural non-profit temple and farm in Montana, Opus Aima Obscuræ, the ladies of the community use scrying mirrors to divine for outcomes and insights during the monthly ladies' dark moon divination rituals. One can also find mirrors on all of our shrines dedicated to Parvati, Lakshmi, Kali, Saraswati, and any other incarnation of Devi Maa (Shakti), the Hindu Mother Goddess. We also adorn the western altar in our temple room with an abundance of mirrors for the elemental association.

In terms of occult practices, mirrors are amplifiers. Because mirrors are reflective, they shine back whatever energy is put into them. If properly enchanted, mirrors will amplify our magick by gathering and reflecting the specific energies we direct toward them. Even the simplest form of spellcraft can benefit from the use of a mirror. By placing a mirror at the center of a Witches' circle, the practitioner can cast specific energies to its surface so that they may bounce outward and radiate into the surrounding area. One may also surround a mirror with magickal tools such as herbs, candles, photos, or whatever other components are needed for a spell; this will amplify the magick that these tools help bring to life. As Mickie has explored, both protection and self-image magick are especially amplified by use of the mirror. Additionally, if a practitioner is working heavily with the element of Water, a circular mirror can be placed within a goblet or bowl of water to amplify the energy and deepen one's connection to the elemental force.

Aside from these uses, one unique way that modern magicians and Witches can utilize mirrors is to dedicate them as otherworldly portals. When I say "otherworldly," I refer to the summoning of forces from alternate planes of reality. Innumerable metaphysical philosophies assert that all planes of existence are accessible and are at least somewhat present here on the earth plane. Because of this, we can imbue mirrors with whatever cosmic or terrestrial energies we choose.

One of the most powerful methods of imbuing a mirror as a portal is to link it with a planetary or zodiacal frequency. One of the easiest ways of accomplishing this is to simply use a marker to draw specific astrological symbols on a small round mirror (I personally love the little $1 bejeweled mirrors from Pier 1). Or, instead of using markers, one may choose to purchase a set of paintbrushes and some glass-etching cream from a craft store; when the cream is painted on a glass surface, it creates a beautiful, powerful "etched" design when it's wiped off. Very magickal indeed!

When mirror-based planetary or zodiacal magick or meditations are performed, the mirror will amplify the energies as a matter of course, especially if that cosmic energy is pronounced on that particular day, such as through the current sun sign, moon sign, planetary retrograde, or astronomical occurrence. It's especially magickal to shine the mirror into the sky toward the direction of the cosmic force you are harnessing (mobile apps such as Sky Map, The Night Sky, and Sky Guide can help with this). If you would like to deepen your work with planetary magick in particular, you may even etch or draw a planetary seal or kamea on the mirror's surface. You may even take it a step further by adhering a planetary metal to the rim of the mirror (iron for Mars, for example). When mirrors are used as amplifiers and as portals, the possibilities are as endless as the practitioner's creative intuition.

Raven Digitalis
**Neopagan priest, DJ, photographer, and author
of *Shadow Magick Compendium, Planetary Spells & Rituals,*
and *Goth Craft* • www.ravendigitalis.com**

A Silvered Mirror Meditation
for Soul Fragment Retrieval

Sometimes when we deal with trauma, fear, or panic in our lives, whether big or small, we can lose little bits of our personal energy field. These bits are known as soul fragments. Another way we can lose soul fragments is when we deny part of ourselves we don't like or that others have shamed us about; we throw that energy away to achieve temporary survival in a sometimes cruel world. Sometimes we even give away part of our self while caring for someone else. There are also people who absorb energy or soul pieces from others, often unintentionally but sometimes on purpose and for many different reasons.

Life has lots of ups and downs, and eventually many people end up feeling like they're missing something at some point. Retrieving missing soul fragments can help you return to your life mission, regain your personal power, and heal your energy system.

Soul fragments are energy, and energy doesn't disappear even if it has been transferred from one place to another. Since that energy started off as part of your own subtle energy, you can locate it, cleanse it, and reunite it with yourself.

The soul fragments lost through trauma, parts you gave away, or that someone else latched onto unintentionally can be retrieved through several methods. Here is one that you can perform through the use of a witch's mirror. In this meditation you use the mirror to help you visualize and reach into the spirit realm. You also use the mirror as a filter to make sure you're only taking on fragments that are best for your greater good so you are not accidentally absorbing anything unwanted.

It should be said that there are shamans and others who specialize in soul retrieval that can help with more serious cases, but this is a great meditation to help you get some of those soul fragments back and start regaining personal power.

This meditation uses a good-sized mirror, at least one that's eleven by fourteen inches in size. Clean the mirror with blessing mirror wash (see chapter 7). Place the mirror where you can sit before it and see your head and shoulders or at least your entire head. Be sure not to cut off the top of your head, as that's where your crown chakra is located; it is your connection to your higher power, and you'll need your higher power to help you access lost soul fragments. You'll also need to sit close enough to the mirror to look deeply into your own eyes.

Sit comfortably and take several deep breaths in through your nose and out through your mouth. Ground and center yourself and completely relax. Once you've reached a relaxed state, gaze deeply into your own eyes; as you do, fill yourself with bright light. Don't break your gaze during this meditation. You will see things in your peripheral vision or in your mind's eye, but your physical eyes should remain focused upon the reflection of your eyes.

Imagine talking to yourself through telepathy to your own reflection, reaching the part of yourself that exists in nonreality. Your statements don't have to be word for word, as I've described here; after all, you are reaching out to yourself. If you do like the wording, you may also record it in your own voice and play it back during the meditation. The conversation should go something like this:

> *You are part of me as I am part of you. You and I*
> *have been through a lot together, and look at how far*
> *we've come, grown, and how much we've learned.*
> *Through that time we have lost bits of our energy:*
> *soul fragments. It's time to call those fragments home.*
> *You are on the looking-glass side and have access*
> *to deep spirit. I ask you to please call back as many*
> *missing soul fragments as you can find. Draw in any*
> *soul fragments whose return will be for our greater*
> *good at this time; invite them from near and far to*
> *come into this light; shake off any pain, anxiety, or*
> *sorrow; and return in peace and love as aligned with*
> *our higher power. Allow this blessed mirror to be*
> *a panacea that helps cleanse our soul fragments of*
> *their difficulties as they return to our open arms.*

Continue to gaze into your own eyes after you've made the request. Your eyes' reflection is your connection to the spirit realm, and you'll find the truth in your own eyes. Through your peripheral vision you might notice a slight glow above the top of your reflection's head. If you glance at it directly it will likely become invisible, but as you stare into your eyes, you'll see it. As the glow becomes stronger, you will see specks of light begin to be drawn in toward your reflection, and you may feel warm energy surrounding you. Greet these specks of light that surround you on both sides of the looking glass: they are your soul fragments, lost little stars now called home. Invite them to rejoin you. Honor each fragment as they reunite with your personal energy field and feel joy at their return.

For several days after this meditation, you should drink plenty of water to bless your spirit and wash away any toxins released as your soul fragments become integrated within your energy system. Once your soul fragments have returned and become fully integrated, you may discover that you've adopted a new attitude and even more healthy behavior patterns. This is a time in your life when you will probably experience a new awakening of your being.

I worked through this meditation years ago, around the time of my divorce from my first husband. That was like a lifetime ago. It was a very empowering experience. I was amazed with the results, which allowed me to grow in the strength that I needed in order to stand up on my own, take care of my daughters, and create a new life for us. Drawing back my soul fragments that I had let go of really brought healing into my life. I'll never forget the pivotal moment standing before that mirror when I saw my own energy radiating out, powerful and healed. I hope this technique will serve you well.

MIRROR LORE
Some traditions include breaking the mirrors of the deceased to keep their spirits from haunting their home.

Mirror Meditations

Dark Mirror Meditation to Enhance Scrying

Scrying is an art that uses a visual image, such as a scrying mirror, as a blank screen powered by your own intuition. One of the time-honored ways to enhance your intuition and improve your psychic abilities is through meditation. This meditation uses your scrying mirror, opening yourself up to deeper intuition while helping your subconscious mind to establish a link between the use of the mirror and your psychic impressions.

The chakra that's responsible for helping us see beyond the physical is the sixth chakra, or third eye chakra. When you just "know" something, have a vision, or get a feeling about a person, a place, or a situation that you can't explain, that's because the psychic input is being processed through the energy vortex in your subtle body known as the third eye chakra. It's located in the center of your forehead, between your physical eyes. This chakra is also associated with your pineal gland, which is a gland deep inside of your brain that is believed to be the center of intuition and psychic abilities. When you open your third eye chakra, you awaken the pineal gland, helping you to access psychic information.

Opening the third eye can really help you tap into all kinds of information that you can't learn through your other physical senses; therefore, it is essential for scrying. What you're seeing in the scrying mirror is actually being seen with your third eye.

Sit before the scrying mirror with the light on so that you can actually see the reflection of your face on the surface of the black mirror. You may anoint your third eye with frankincense, sandalwood, or clary sage essential oil, if you wish, and hold an amethyst, lepidolite, or kyanite stone over your third eye for a few minutes.

Now relax your body and gaze at your reflection within the black scrying mirror, focusing on your third eye and breathing deeply in through your nose and out through your mouth. As you do so, relax your gaze. Now imagine a bluish-violet colored light emanating from the center of your forehead. The light begins to unfold slowly, much like the blooming of a flower. You may feel like pressure is building up behind your third eye; it will release as it opens. As you feel the third eye open, speak the mantra *om* and draw it out into a long breath. The next several outbreaths should include a long, drawn-out *ohm*. Now visualize two winglike petals extending on either side across your brow, over your physical eyes. Allow the sparkling flower of light to glow and pulse with light.

If you try this technique and struggle to visualize it in the black scrying mirror, you may simply close your eyes, if that helps. Visualization can take practice; remember, there is no right or wrong way—do what works!

Now you have taken your first step on the road to empowering your third eye, which will bring deeper intuition. Feel free to repeat this exercise anytime you feel you need to, especially before scrying.

Mirror Gazing to See Your Aura

Everyone has an energy field around their bodies; we call it an aura. What's the point of seeing your aura, you may ask? The size, shape, and colors in your aura can be a good indicator of things like mood or watching for energy depletion. It's great to know your own energy. When you learn to see your own aura, you may be able to see other people's auras too. This is a nice way to get some extra insight into many situations with people and their interactions, motivations, and more. Some people are visual clairvoyants and can see auras without any practice, while other people who want to see auras can learn to see them by practicing.

I actually practiced this technique when I was in middle school during the 1970s. I was really interested in anything paranormal—I never missed an episode of *In Search of…*, and I even found a book about dreams and dream interpretation in the Scholastic catalog, intrepid little witchling that I was! I discovered a technique for how to see auras somewhere in between watching specials about the Bermuda Triangle and reading *Chariots of the Gods*. (Yep, I was a weird kid—no big surprise there!)

Anyway, people have been practicing this technique for learning to view auras in the mirror for ages, and now I'll share it with you. While I have been able to see auras on occasion, more often I sense auras, feeling that someone has a pleasant or energetic or greasy or soothing aura but not always seeing them in a physical way. I began doing this meditation again while I was working on this book, and I must say it's a great exercise to revisit. With practice, I'm having some success again; I hope you do too.

Stand in front of a mirror. Your bathroom mirror works fine for this exercise, but if you want to have a special mirror for this purpose, that's actually a great idea. For the best results a white wall behind you is best, especially if you're new at this. A plain white wall is less distracting and can help you discover your aura much easier than on a wall with patterns or a wide-open room with many textures and patterns. If you don't have a mirror with a white wall in the reflection behind you, grab a white sheet and pin it up behind you.

Begin by gazing deeply into your own eyes. As you do, ask your spirit guides, higher power, or a god or goddess that you work with frequently to assist you in seeing your aura. Now soften your gaze slightly and shift your vision to the center of your forehead, between your eyes (remember, where your

235
. . .
Mirror Meditations

third eye chakra is). Some people have an easier time using the edge of your body, such as where your neck meets your shoulder, as a focal point, so feel free to try both and discover what works best for you. Try to stare as long as you can; you'll only be able to do it for a few minutes at a time—it's kind of like trying to see one of those magic eye images, which I personally have a terrible time seeing, though when I can see them, it's awesome!

Eventually you should see a thin, white, hazy glow or a transparent-looking energy extending just past your body— that's your inner aura, the energy field that surrounds you and fills your being. If you try to look at it directly it's likely that it will disappear, so be sure to keep your gaze soft and relaxed. If you get really excited and lose it, don't feel bad; this is just the first step in the right direction. It does take a lot of practice, but eventually it's likely that as you start to move your vision outward, you'll start to see colors extending past the white inner aura. Many people have even been able to see faces from their past lives or experience the energies of guides surrounding them.

You can practice this for a few minutes a couple times a week. The more you do it, the better you'll get at seeing energy.

Scrying Symbols

A dream dictionary is a good way to familiarize yourself with the symbols of the subconscious mind, but always remember that some symbols have different meanings for different people. Those of us who are witches can also look to our own set of symbolism that we use regularly, such as rune shapes or ogham symbols, tarot symbolism, Lenormand, or tea-reading symbols that are already part of our subconscious mind. One person might see a letter B and consider it an initial, but a witch who uses runes frequently might recognize it as the rune Beorc, a symbol of health, love, and life force. A bird might suggest a message from your higher power, but if you've been working with Lenormand oracle decks a lot, you might interpret several birds as more mundane communication, phone calls, negotiations, or gossip.

More often than not, you'll see clouds or sometimes symbols when scrying; it's really different for different people. The important thing to remember is that allowing the visions to come is really not a matter of trying really, really hard. The more relaxed and less uptight about it you are, the easier it will get, and that is something that comes with time.

The appendices in this book are guides for interpreting the most common images and basic visions you may encounter while scrying in your witch's mirror. Keep in mind that while many symbols follow standard archetypes, some can mean different things to different people, so if any of the interpretations I've included don't ring true for you, feel free to alter them to fit within your own mental and spiritual framework. Consider this just a jumping-off point.

Take your time and relax. Soften your focus not on the surface of the mirror but through it to the other side, and let it flow. Be sure to jot down any impressions you might have—just quick notes that you can make without breaking your gaze or right after you finish. Transfer these quickly written notes into a scrying journal. This helps you keep track of your progress and also can help you verify things seen in the mirror as they come up in the everyday world.

Conclusion

Reflections Upon
the Witch's Mirror

Before I first began doing research for this book, I had a handful of some pretty good ideas for magic using mirrors since I've been including different kinds of mirrors on and off in my magical practice for years. I welcomed the opportunity to share what I've learned so far as well as discover new ways to work with mirrors. Researching a project is a lot like opening presents to me, as I revel in learning something new; I'm betting you love learning new stuff too. I hope that some of the ideas in this book have helped you look at mirror magic with new eyes. After all, mirrors are all about getting a different perspective.

We witches are always discovering that facing our shadow side helps us to grow, so even if we did scare ourselves half to death with Bloody Mary as a kid, we have learned to see beyond that. We witches walk between the worlds, torch in hand illuminating the path before us, tipping our faces up to that silvery mirror in the sky and embracing things we didn't understand as children while making them our own.

On the other hand, there are many people who see mirrors as purely scientific apparatus that reflect light, direct lasers, and help us see the bigger picture. Some see only a tool for beauty; for them, the scariest thing in the mirror is a bad hair day or new crow's feet. Many use mirrors as a tool for self-improvement; big wall mirrors in exercise classes are so we can check our stance, our pose, and make sure we're doing what we should be. Some people see mirrors as an element of decoration used to brighten up a space, reflect a pretty view, or make a room magically appear larger. Mirrors are all these things, but they are also much more.

When we look beyond the mirror as a tool for reflecting our physical being or as an object of pure superstition, we discover what it really is. It is something in between those two perceptions. When we realize that, the mirror becomes a tool to help us rediscover our own personal worth and our spiritual side, an object to inspire introspection like no other. A mirror becomes a magical tool of great value.

. . .
Conclusion

The word *reflection* describes more than just the physical property of a mirror. Reflection is also a word that we use to describe what happens when we look within and remind ourselves of our spiritual nature, the significance of our path, and our place in the universe.

I hope that you learned a lot within the pages of this book. When you gaze upon your own reflection within your witch's mirror, may you see all the beauty, magic, and potential that resides behind your powerful magical eyes, and may you become inspired to work with a witch's mirror or two along your magical path.

> *Mirror, mirror of the witch*
> *Bless my magic full and rich*
> *Show to me your secret light*
> *Bless my spirit both day and night*

Blessed be!

Mickie Mueller

Acknowledgments

My thanks go out to many people who helped make this book possible: my husband, Dan, the wind beneath my wings and the fire beneath my butt who keeps my creative brain on task, and my son, Tristan, kept the home fires burning while I sat and worked for long hours at a time. They listened to my crazy ideas, proofread, and encouraged me to keep going. Also thanks to my daughters, Brittany and Chelsea, for cheering me on from afar so I could keep working; with girls like them, they're never far at all. Thanks to my mom and Papa Gecko for proofreading my proposal. Oh, and Mom—thanks for the old family mirror from the farm; it's a treasure! Thanks to my dad for all the art gallery memories, which inspired my mirror washes and purifier, and also for teaching me your excellent framing skills that work as well for mirrors as they do for art.

Thanks to my wonderful editors, Elysia Gallo and Rebecca Zins, for diligently keeping me on the right track, answering my newb questions, and skillfully making a book out of a manuscript; to Lynne Menturweck, art director extraordinaire, for helping me juggle writing and illustration deadlines successfully; may your jar of M&Ms never be empty. Also thanks to everyone at Llewellyn, especially Bill Krause, Nanette Stearns, Tom Lund, and Vanessa Wright for making it all happen. Thanks to Deborah Blake for setting the standard for this series with her wonderful and inspiring book *The Witch's Broom* and for being awesome in general. A special thanks to John Kachik, not only for the charming cover art for this book, but for all the covers for this whole series; your cover art was always close at hand and inspired me as I did the interiors for this book and the rest of the series. You rock!

My undying gratitude goes to Willow the cat for allowing me to borrow her cat-warming machine with all the funny lettered buttons with which to write this book.

Thanks to my friends on social media and in person who got excited and encouraged me even when I had to keep the title and topic of this book under wraps.

And last but certainly not least, thanks to all of the wonderful witchy authors who contributed their knowledge and personal stories in the "Reflections of Real Witches" segments. These authors lent so much insight and inspiration, and I was honored to have each and every one be a part of this book! Please check out their other works, dear reader; you won't be disappointed.

Appendix 1

The Symbolism of Color

When you practice scrying in a black mirror, often you will see clouds of color instead of actual symbols. These clouds can be very powerful ways to receive messages if you know how to read them. The movements or positions of these clouds when scrying can be an indicator of the energies. If the clouds move toward the right, it can mean that your spirit guides or higher powers are at work assisting you. If the clouds are on the left side or moving toward the left, the answers you seek might still be unfolding and under influences that cannot yet be known. If upon asking a specific question the clouds seem to move up and forward, toward you, that is a positive response. If upon asking a question the clouds seem to move downward and away from you, that is a no or negative response.

Sometimes clouds are the most you'll get when scrying, but with practice some people are able to see images—clouds in the shapes of things or images that are even more clear. If you think you see shapes in the clouds or get stronger visions, the second appendix of scrying symbols might also be helpful. If symbols you see appear in a certain color, that should also be noted and cross-referenced in your interpretations. Always keep in mind that your personal feelings and impressions are very important while interpreting what you see in your scrying mirror.

Black: Black can be a warning to be cautious in the situation you're seeking an answer to. It also can mean something hidden, endings, or something waning. Black can be a powerful color for protection.

Blue: Peace, honor, and friendship are at hand. Tranquil energies surround the situation; the color can also indicate faith or legal situations.

Green: Growth and abundance have long been associated with green. Finances, money, and harmony with nature are represented by green.

Orange: This color stands for pride, accolades, and self-esteem.

Pink: Romance and matters of the heart. Faithful love or even love of the self.

Purple: Spirituality and strength of psychic growth, mysticism, and enlightenment.

Red: Red can point to courage, willpower, or sexual passion, but it can also be a warning of anger or danger of some kind. Pay attention to how you feel when you see it.

White or Gray: Seeing white or gray clouds is a positive sign for the future and can indicate good luck and the influence of the divine goddess in the situation. A white or gray mist is sometimes the first thing you'll see, opening the way to visions.

Yellow: Usually indicates intellectual matters, creativity, or optimistic outlooks, but on some occasions yellow can indicate caution.

The Symbolism of Color

Appendix 2

Scrying Symbols

Airplane: Travel is in the future. Observe the plane's actions to indicate the situation surrounding any upcoming travel plans.

Anchor: Settling on something. Security. A successful journey or project is secure.

Angel or Faerie: Good news is coming. Blessings.

Apple: Good health. Love. Good luck in achieving your goal.

Arrow: Bad news is coming to you—a problem you need to deal with.

Basket: A present. A surprise. Something good and unexpected.

Bat: Complications may arise due to someone else's interference.

Bear: Solid finances. A mentor who may be able to assist you.

Bed: A time of rest is needed; heed this advice to keep your health.

Bell: A wedding in the future. A partnership or a wake-up call.

Bird: Messenger of the gods. Good luck. Possibly travel or communication.

Bridge: A crossing from one area of life to another. Also may indicate overcoming an obstacle.

Broom: Cleanse your surroundings; you may need to get rid of what no longer serves you.

Butterfly: Growth. Becoming more than you are. Transformation.

Car: Your journey in life. Pay attention to where you're steering. Be ready for changes.

Cat: Be careful of who you confide in; others might not be who they appear to be.

Circle: Success. Oneness. Can also indicate things going in cycles.

Clover: Good fortune. Luck is going your way.

Cross: Difficulties. A sign of misfortune or a situation involving a sacrifice of some kind.

Crown: Success. Achieving your goals. Recognition for all your hard work.

Cup: Can represent family bloodlines or a blessing of honor.

Dagger: A warning of danger or loss.

Dog: A loyal friend—someone you can rely on.

Door: A new chapter unfolding. An opportunity for a big change.

Dragon: Inner strength to take on something new.

Egg: Something new. A positive sign.

Eye: Consciousness—if open, awakening; if closed, something that is unseen.

Feather: Soaring spiritually. Ascension.

Fish: Joy. Bounty. Good health.

Flag: Standing your ground against opposition.

Flower or Flowers: Love. Happiness. An unexpected gift.

Gate: A solution to a problem is at hand. An opportunity for success.

Goat: Be careful of people you know are your enemies.

Gun: Anger; try to avoid conflict. A gun can also be a phallic symbol.

Scrying Symbols

Hammer: Hard work ahead will pay off. The need to drive a point home.

Hand: Help from someone or you will be helping someone.

Heart: A relationship being restored or growing deeper.

Hourglass: Make a decision—time is running out.

Ivy: Overcoming obstacles. Grace under pressure.

Key: You have the power to succeed. Unlock doors.

Kite: A wish comes true.

Ladder: Advancement or promotion. Gaining status. May also point to DNA, or your nature.

Leaf: Renewed hope. A new beginning.

Mouse: Problems arise—little annoyances, possibly theft.

Nail: Sometimes life isn't fair. An injustice you must deal with.

Octopus: Dangerous situation. Spreading yourself too thin, multitasking too much.

Owl: Beware of gossip. Watch for health problems and take action.

Paintbrush: Creative energy. Creating a harmonious situation.

Pig: Achieving honors and abundance. Can also symbolize greed.

Question Mark: Proceed with caution—more information is needed.

Rabbit: The need to be brave. May also represent renewal and fertility.

Ring: Marriage or partnership. Commitment. Cycles.

Scissors: Cutting off something. Arguments.

Ship: Travel. An unexpected journey. Your ship coming in.

Spider: Communication. Connectivity to everything around you.

Star: Happiness. Health. A symbol of hope. A positive sign.

Tornado: Things being shaken up. Big changes ahead. Hardship.

Tree: Good health. Improvement of a situation. Your life path.

Umbrella: Help is coming your way.

Volcano: Volatile emotions boiling over.

Wasp: Problems with romance. Battling others about your relationship.

Wheel: Good luck. Work within the cycles, not against them. Moving forward.

Wings: Watch for messages—could mean email, letters, or even messages from Spirit.

Scrying Symbols

Zigzag: Erratic behavior. Defensive behavior.

Zodiac: Look for traits of any zodiac signs you see. Can also point to timing.

Recommended Reading

Here are some books with more information about the enchanted witch's mirror as well as general magic and witch-craft. Most of these were used as reference material while researching this book. I hope you find the books on this list intriguing and inspiring.

Bardon, Franz. *Initiation into Hermetics: A Course of Instruction of Magic Theory & Practice.* Merkur Publishing, 2013; Kindle edition.

Cunningham, Scott. *Cunningham's Encyclopedia of Magical Herbs,* expanded and revised edition. St. Paul: Llewellyn, 2000.

Dugan, Ellen. *Garden Witch's Herbal: Green Magick, Herbalism & Spirituality.* Woodbury: Llewellyn, 2009.

Gaiman, Neil, and Dave McKean. *MirrorMask*. New York: HarperCollins Publishers, 2005.

Grant, Ember. *The Book of Crystal Spells: Magical Uses for Stones, Crystals, Minerals, and Even Sand*. Woodbury: Llewellyn, 2013.

Illes, Judika. *The Element Encyclopedia of 1000 Spells: A Concise Reference Book for the Magical Arts*. London: Harper Element, 2010.

———. *The Element Encyclopedia of Witchcraft: The Complete A–Z for the Entire Magical World*. London: Harper Element, 2005.

Lennox, Michael. *Llewellyn's Complete Dictionary of Dreams: Over 1,000 Dream Symbols and Their Universal Meanings*. Woodbury: Llewellyn, 2015.

Melchior-Bonnet, Sabine. *The Mirror: A History*. New York: Routledge, 2001.

Morrison, Dorothy. *Everyday Magic*. St. Paul: Llewellyn, 1998.

Nelson, John. *The Magic Mirror: Divination Through the Ancient Art of Scrying*. Bookworks Publishing LTD; Kindle edition.

Penczak, Christopher. *The Temple of High Witchcraft: Ceremonies, Spheres, and the Witches' Qabalah*. Woodbury: Llewellyn, 2007.

Pendergrast, Mark. *Mirror, Mirror: A History of the Human Love Affair with Reflection*. New York: Perseus Books; Kindle edition.

Randolph, Paschal Beverly. *Seership: Guide to Soul Sight and the Magic Mirror and How to Use It*. Quakertown: The Confederation of Initiates, 1930.

Randolph, Vance. *Ozark Magic and Folklore*. New York: Dover Publications, 1964.

Tyson, Donald. *How to Make and Use a Magic Mirror—Psychic Windows into New Worlds*. St. Paul: Llewellyn, 1990.

Valiente, Doreen. *An ABC of Witchcraft*. Custer: Phoenix Publishing, 1973.

———. *Charge of the Goddess*. East Sussex: Hexagon Hoopix, 2000.

Weschcke, Carl Llewellyn, and Joe H. Slate, PhD. *Communicating with Spirit*. Woodbury: Llewellyn, 2015.

———. *The Llewellyn Complete Book of Psychic Empowerment*. Woodbury: Llewellyn, 2011.

Whitehurst, Tess. *Magical Housekeeping: Simple Charms & Practical Tips for Creating a Harmonious Home*. Woodbury: Llewellyn, 2010.

Websites of Interest

Kate Fox, "Mirror, Mirror: A Summary of Research Findings on Body Image," S.I.R.C. Social Issues Research Center, 1 January 1997, http://www.sirc.org/publik/mirror.html

Ian Mursell, "See and Be Seen: ('Smoking') Mirrors," Aztecs at Mexicolore, http://www.mexicolore.co.uk/aztecs/artefacts/smoking-mirrors

Bryan Nelson, "Crows Use Mirrors to Hunt for Food," Mother Nature Network, 21 September 2011, http://www.mnn.com/earth-matters/animals/stories/crows-use-mirrors-to-hunt-for-food

Index

To Write to the Author

If you wish to contact the author or would like more information about this book, please write to the author in care of Llewellyn Worldwide and we will forward your request. Both the author and the publisher appreciate hearing from you and learning of your enjoyment of this book and how it has helped you. Llewellyn Worldwide cannot guarantee that every letter written to the author can be answered, but all will be forwarded. Please write to:

Mickie Mueller

Llewellyn Worldwide

2143 Wooddale Drive

Woodbury, MN 55125-2989

Please enclose a self-addressed stamped envelope for reply
or $1.00 to cover costs. If outside the USA, enclose
an international postal reply coupon.

Many of Llewellyn's authors have websites with additional information and resources. For more information, please visit our website:

WWW.LLEWELLYN.COM